WAINWRIGHT
IN THE
LIMESTONE DALES

WAINWRIGHT
IN THE
LIMESTONE DALES

with photographs by
ED GELDARD

GUILD PUBLISHING
LONDON · NEW YORK · SYDNEY · TORONTO

This edition published 1991 by Guild Publishing
by arrangement with MICHAEL JOSEPH LTD

Copyright © Text 1991 by A. Wainwright
Copyright © Photographs 1991 by Ed Geldard
Copyright © Frontispiece map 1991 by Chris Jesty
Copyright © Other maps and line drawings 1970 Westmorland Gazette

A CIP catalogue record for this book is available from the British Library

CN 1319

Typeset in 10½ on 13pt Linotron Ehrhardt
by Goodfellow & Egan Phototypesetters Ltd., Cambridge
Colour origination by Anglia Graphics, Bedford
Printed and bound in The Netherlands by Royal Smeets Offset B.V., Weert

The moral right of the author has been asserted

CONTENTS

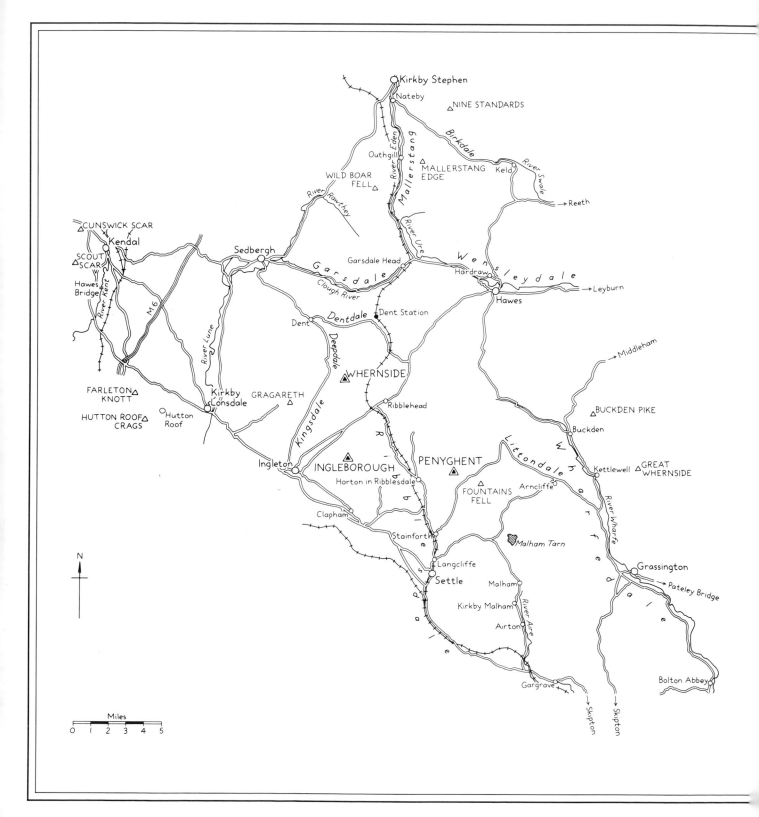

INTRODUCTION

Some twenty years ago I wrote a guidebook to the walks on and around the three peaks of Ingleborough, Penyghent and Whernside in Upper Ribblesdale, supplementing the text with over two hundred pen-and-ink drawings. The book proved very popular but I was left with a nagging regret that my limitations with a camera had prevented me from portraying the district in colour. Black-and-white drawings could not convey even a remote impression of the emerald greenery of these wonderful hills nor the vast skyscapes and panoramic views seen from their summits. I had failed miserably to give my readers a true picture of the visual delights awaiting those who followed in my footsteps. The area deserved a better treatment: I had not done justice to a part of northern England where I had wandered as a youngster and often visited later, developing an affection that has persisted into old age. Memories of happy days on the hills never fade but cannot be shared with others through the medium of the written word as effectively as colourful pictures.

It was a godsend when Ed Geldard, a professional photographer and enthusiastic walker, came to settle in Kendal from the north-east. He proved to be the answer to my long-standing wish that someone would come along who could show in pictures the scenes where I had found beauty and interest and wanted others to see. We teamed up. I came out of slippered retirement and enjoyed a late bonus by visiting the old familiar places once again – but this time with a master cameraman. So good was his work, so fulfilling of my ambitions, that I have been well content to let my narrative in this book play second fiddle to his excellent photographs. I have put pen to paper sparingly, aware that pictures speak louder than words. This is Ed's book more than it is mine.

It was so nice for me to renew acquaintance once again with my old and trusted friends, Ingleborough and Company. They were as welcoming as ever; a little surprised because they had thought I had forsaken them. In a world of rapid change they never change. They were just as I remembered them. I commend them, and the area over which they preside, to adventurers and explorers of all ages, and especially to sufferers from urban depression for which they are the perfect tonic. Life always seems good in the company of the Three Peaks.

I have omitted, with reluctance, references to a few natural features of interest that have been subject to abuse of privilege by a minority of visitors. I have had complaints from farmers of accumulations of litter in places where sheep graze, of the fouling of streams that provide the drinking water for farms, of the erosion of footpaths caused by parties walking abreast on paths intended for single-file walking, and of the crossing of private farmland without permission being sought. I have written this book only for visitors who behave responsibly and show respect for others.

I am grateful to the Dalesman Publishing Co. Ltd. for their kind permission to reproduce illustrations of Cave Systems from their publications, and add my tribute to the excellent work of the cartographer Mr G.M. Davies.

1 SOME NORTHERN HIGHLIGHTS

THE AREA TO BE described in this book lies mainly in the north-west corner of Yorkshire where the Three Peaks of Ingleborough, Penyghent and Whernside rise steeply from a compact bedrock of limestone between Dentdale and Malham.

To the north of the area isolated tracts of limestone intrude among the peaty gritstones of the Pennines, adding a sparkle to the sombre landscapes by erupting on the surface in natural features and formations that demand attention: some are easily accessible and are popular objectives attracting many visitors, while others are little known and reached only by walking over rough ground.

The most interesting of these natural features are detailed in this chapter.

Mallerstang Valley

FELL END CLOUDS

Travellers on the road between Sedbergh and Kirkby Stephen, the A683, pass through attractive countryside of contrasting landscapes, all fair to look upon and with few habitations to counter the loneliness of the surroundings. At the southern end, the road follows the valley of the River Rawthey along the base of the Howgill Fells, seen intimately in colourful array and having a highlight in Cautley Spout where waterfalls plunge 800 feet down a steep fellside; east of the road are the sprawling slopes of Baugh Fell. This section is lovely, with the river, rich pastures and native trees blending in rural harmony, a peaceful scene emphasised by the wild hills on both sides.

Beyond Rawthey Bridge, where the river changes direction, the road gradually enters a different terrain, more open and bare, the last few miles crossing a bleak moorland overlooked by Wild Boar Fell and its northern ridge. Despite its classification as an A road, it is relatively quiet and only an occasional car will disturb a walker's appreciation of the scenery. I once walked, or rather limped, the thirteen miles of tarmac, plagued by a protruding nail in the sole of my shoe which was digging a small crater in my heel, and during the whole journey not a single vehicle passed me. But that was a long time ago, before the war.

Midway, a loop road branches from the A683 and runs at a higher level before rejoining it two and a half miles further on. This byroad was formerly the main highway; it is now little used although it is kept in good repair to serve the few local farmsteads. It is still known as The Street and, after rejoining the A683, again departs from it at the site of an old toll bar, branching off as a rough track to visit the hamlet of Stennerskeugh. It then continues north to be overlaid finally by the main road on Kirkby Stephen Common. Approaching from Sedbergh, The Street turns off to the right immediately after crossing Rawthey Bridge and climbs steeply before contouring, with excellent views denied to the motorist on the

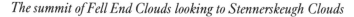

The summit of Fell End Clouds looking to Stennerskeugh Clouds

A683, alongside a moorland pockmarked with shake-holes. These are sure signs of a limestone bedrock, and this is soon confirmed by two limekilns in an open field, both long disused but remaining almost intact.

At this point attention will be drawn, especially on a sunny day, to the white capping of the fell rising beyond the kilns, having the appearance of a cloud clinging to the crest. This is a mile-long limestone scar, given the name of Fell End Clouds by the imaginative early settlers in the district. There is a counterpart to the north known as Stennerskeugh Clouds. Both names have been preserved by the Ordnance Survey on their maps.

The traverse of Fell End Clouds is a short delightful expedition, less than three miles in walking distance from the road and entailing only 500 feet of climbing. It is happily served by two old paths for ascent and descent, encouraging a circular walk best done clockwise. Two hours is ample time, but walkers with interests in botany, geology or archaeology will be sorely tempted to linger.

Few people nowadays prefer to walk to their objective if they can be carried on wheels, and Fell End Clouds is so remote from centres of population that visitors invariably arrive by car. There is parking space in a disused quarry alongside The Street near its junction with the A683.

The walk starts at a gate in the roadside wall at this junction, opposite a copse of trees marking an old Quaker burial ground. The gate admits to a path, presumably made as a droveway for bringing sheep down from the fell; this spirals up to the ridge where a turn to the right leads to the summit cairn. It will now be seen that the escarpment is the abrupt end of a large plateau culminating in Wild Boar Fell. The descent to the south passes the relics of an abandoned lead mine and arrives at Clouds Gill to join the old mine road which goes down past the limekilns to The Street and the waiting car.

Above *A limekiln near The Street*
Below *The old mine workings*

WILD BOAR FELL

Wild Boar Fell rises to 2324 feet above the sea and is the dominant height between the Lake District and the main Pennine range, overlooking the nearby Howgill Fells and all else for many miles around. The distinctive profile of the eastern edge of the summit is a feature instantly recognised in the landscape of the upper Eden valley. It overlooks the birthplace of the lovely River Eden and nurtures and shelters its flow down the long strath of Mallerstang towards an ultimate destination in the Solway Firth.

The fell is reputedly the last place in England where a wild boar was killed, hence the name, and has other claims to distinction. A tumulus on the summit ridge is evidence that it was known, probably as a hunting ground, and may indeed have been occupied as a settlement by primitive man. Nearer our own time, millstones were fashioned from the gritstone rocks of the upper slopes for the many water-powered mills in the district, and debris of this industry may still be found by diligent search near Sand Tarn. And along the base of the fell runs the highest railway in the country, the famous Settle to Carlisle line.

Geologically, the fell has a dual character. Although capped by gritstone and having a fringe of cliffs that have been largely shattered into wastes of boulders and scree, there is an extensive intrusion of limestone at mid-height on both flanks. On the west side are the twin escarpments of Fell End Clouds and Stennerskeugh Clouds, and on the east a broad shelf is pitted by a long line of shakeholes and potholes, the Angerholme Pots. On this side too is the spectacular ravine of White Kirk on Ais Gill, a limestone gorge of impressive proportions; it is Wild Boar's greatest showplace.

Wild Boar Fell

The circuit of Wild Boar Fell is a splendid expedition on rough ground and without the help of trodden paths. The walk is best done anti-clockwise, starting from the B6259 near the head of the valley of Mallerstang. Cars may be parked in an old quarry near the railway bridge. I remember the time when two sheep-dogs were daily tethered at this bridge, one at each side, to deter sheep from wandering on the road from the open fell: a sort of canine cattle grid.

The road is left further on, when abreast of Aisgill Farm. A track on the left passes under a railway viaduct, where the temptation to visit the ravine of White Kirk directly ahead should be resisted until the return journey; instead, turn right to join and follow a wall along the fellside and, when it turns down, cross the gently rising limestone plateau ahead. Here are the Angerholme Pots, all lined up for inspection over a straight half-mile. At the end, a steep scramble leads up to a depression in the north ridge of the fell. Now the objective is a prominent height to the left; this is The Nab, crowned by a cairn that marks the site of a prehistoric tumulus.

Below *The Nab*　　　　　　　　　　　　　　　　　Above *Angerholme Pots*

Above *The summit cairn*

Below *Sand Tarn*

The Nab is an excellent viewpoint, better in fact than the actual summit of Wild Boar Fell although of lower elevation. The sharp declivities on all sides give depth to the prospect and reveal Mallerstang below and the Eden valley winding into the distance backed by Cross Fell, with the town of Kirkby Stephen also easily seen.

From The Nab, it is a short walk to the summit, marked by an Ordnance Survey column that fits snugly into a stone wind shelter. Here the view is slightly more extensive but the broad top hides all valley details. The peaks of Ingleborough and Whernside are prominent southwards, and Great Shunner Fell and Lovely Seat in the Pennines eastwards, but the gem of the panorama is the serrated skyline of the Lakeland fells overtopping the Howgills and forming an exciting western horizon. Below the summit on the west side is Sand Tarn, well known to the millstone workers of old but rarely visited today.

Descent is made southwards over a pathless moor to a depression containing a small tarn and a wall that rises to the next height, Swarth Fell. From this depression, the descent is continued down the Mallerstang flank, soon linking with Ais Gill coming down from Wild Boar Fell. The stream can be followed down towards the railway viaduct, the drab surroundings being suddenly and unexpectedly relieved when the stream, innocuous thus far, plunges over the edge of a limestone gorge. This is White Kirk, a secret place hidden from the sight of those who pass along Mallerstang but known to botanists for its plants and mosses. The stream, now lively and excited, splashes over fallen rocks between high ramparts.

A little lower down the fellside, the stream falls into another ravine, Low White Kirk, and flows more sedately under the viaduct and the road to join the River Eden. Walkers too must pass under the viaduct to return to their starting point on the road.

Low White Kirk, Ais Gill

MALLERSTANG

Mallerstang is one of the quietest of the Pennine valleys, unfrequented by tourists and free from heavy traffic: it is a pleasant ribbon of green deepset between lofty heights, sparsely populated and always giving the impression of rural contentment and a way of life that remains as unchanged as the landscape. The valley has a long history of fact and legend, and age has mellowed its few buildings. The pervading aura of peace was interrupted only in the early 1870s when an army of men carved a railway throughout its length, since when an undisturbed tranquillity has prevailed. Yet there is much of scenic and historic interest here to delight the leisurely visitor.

The B6259 road into Mallerstang from the south leaves the Sedbergh—Hawes road at the Moorcock Inn near Garsdale Head in a setting of bleak moorland, and rises gently, with the railway coming alongside, to Aisgill Moor Cottages, a terrace of humble dwellings built for the workers responsible for maintaining this highest of English railways which here attains its summit at 1169 feet. For many years after the war, these cottages were unoccupied and were offered for sale at a thousand pounds each, with no takers; they have since been acquired as holiday homes. In the field opposite are fissures in the underlying limestone, entrances to long subterranean passages. Of much greater significance, however, is the skyline of the fells rising to the east, where above the 2000-ft contour and barely a mile apart two important rivers have their beginnings – the Eden, destined to flow north to the Solway Firth, and the Ure, bound eastwards for Wensleydale and ultimately the North Sea.

From Aisgill Summit, the railway, the road and the River Eden go hand in hand down Mallerstang, forced into close company by the impending slopes, and almost at once there appears on the right the magnificent spectacle of Hellgill Force where the infant Eden, thus far known as Hell Gill Beck, leaps in a waterfall of 60 feet over a limestone cliff and comes to maturity as the River Eden. You can reach the waterfall by a lane leaving the road at the cottages.

Hellgill Force

A short mile further on, the road passes over the stream, Ais Gill, issuing from the impressive limestone confines of White Kirk, hidden by the railway viaduct and unseen and unsuspected from the road which continues uneventfully down the valley and arrives at the compact little community of Outhgill. Here is the modest parish church of St Mary: the date of its founding is obscure, but a panel over the porch records that the building was restored by Lady Anne Clifford in 1663 after she found it in ruinous condition.

Beyond Outhgill, in a field on the left, is the gaunt ruin of Pendragon Castle. The origins of this ancient structure are lost in antiquity: according to legend it replaced a fifth-century fortress occupied by Uther Pendragon, a man of great influence and supposedly the father of King Arthur. There appears to be substance in the legend by the surviving name of the castle, and there is further support in a couplet that still lives on, referring to his abortive attempt to divert the course of the river to surround the fortress as a moat:

> Let Uther Pendragon do what he can,
> Eden will run where Eden ran.

Since early days, the castle has been laid waste and rebuilt many times before being inherited by the great benefactress, Lady Anne Clifford, who restored it in 1660. However, the next owner dismantled the walls in 1685, since when it has remained in a state of decay.

Mallerstang loses its identity after passing Pendragon, the Eden flowing resolutely north through more open countryside of low hills terraced by the lynchets of the early settlers. The derelict fourteenth-century Lammerside Castle and the stately Wharton Hall, a fine example of a late medieval house built for defence with an imposing gateway, are passed on the west bank before reaching the more sylvan surroundings of the village of Nateby and the environs of the pleasant market town of Kirkby Stephen.

Pendragon Castle

Mallerstang Edge

MALLERSTANG EDGE

The valley of Mallerstang is bound on the east throughout its length by a continuous range of fells consistently above the 2000-ft contour and scarped by cliffs in many places along its crest. The range is geographically important since it forms part of the main watershed of northern England. An invisible county boundary, a meeting of Cumbria and North Yorkshire, follows the height of land over many miles of utterly wild and desolate terrain. This is Mallerstang Edge, providing an exhilarating walk unhindered by walls and fences.

The Edge is most easily reached from the top of the B6270 road linking Kirkby Stephen and Keld. This lonely spot, at nearly 1700 feet, I call Birkdale Summit in the absence of an official name, the long valley of Birkdale going down from this point to Keld. If approaching from Kirkby Stephen, as is usual, a halt should be made at Stenkrith Bridge for a look over the parapets at the River Eden below, thrashing a passage through a deep limestone gorge. At Nateby, the road to Keld turns out of the village to spiral upwards to the top of the pass with good views of Mallerstang Edge during the ascent. Cars may be parked on Birkdale Summit which is crossed by both the county boundary and the watershed.

The walk to be described may most conveniently be undertaken by two parties, each with transport: one car should be parked at the roadside quarry at Aisgill, and the other at Birkdale Summit. The two parties walk in opposite directions and exchange car keys as they pass midway or, better still, at a rendezvous at the conspicuous landmark of Lady's Pillar.

Starting from Birkdale Summit, an initial detour may be made to look into the open shaft of Jingling Pot nearby, after which a pathless course must be steered south-west across tedious grass to reach and climb the rough slopes building up to the Edge. The first cairned top, High Pike Hill, is then quickly attained and soon the rim of cliffs trends due south, giving direction to the walk and providing aerial views of Mallerstang below. Peat hags, typical of the Pennine uplands and indicating a gritstone base, mark the way but the walking is easy to the next prominent top, High Seat, at 2328 feet the highest point on the range. Beyond, the Edge becomes less well defined and is succeeded by steep slopes, surmounted by inclining eastwards and following the county boundary and the watershed and keeping always to the height of land in surroundings of utter desolation yet of profound influence on the landscape, for three major rivers have their source hereabouts: the streams flowing east are tributaries of the River Swale, those to the west drain an area known as Eden Springs, the source of the River Eden, and a short distance to the south are the beginnings of the River Ure.

The next felltop reached is Hugh Seat, 2257 feet, the turning point of the walk: high ground continues but then gradually declines into Wensleydale.

Hugh Seat is readily identified by a neat column of cut stones near the summit. This is Lady's Pillar, erected in 1664 on the instructions of Lady Anne Clifford as a memorial to a friend, Sir Hugh Morville, after whom the fell is named. One of the stones is inscribed AP 1664, another has the initials and date FHL 1890: this was the year when the pillar was rebuilt following its collapse.

A descent of the western slope over rough ground leads to a confluence of streams that now goes forward as Hell Gill Beck, still forming the county boundary and being accompanied by a track as it heads south-west. Limestone reappears and is much in evidence when Hellgill Bridge is reached, this centuries-old structure spanning a deep gorge. The bridge carries the old road between Hawes and Kirkby Stephen, superseded in 1825 by the valley road and now grass-grown and neglected but still traceable down to the road near Outhgill if transport is waiting there. According to legend, Dick Turpin leaped across the gorge here on his horse Black Bess on a journey to or from York, presumably before the bridge was built.

If Aisgill is the destination the track is followed down below the bridge alongside the gorge to arrive at Hellgill Farm, from where an access road goes down to the B6259 at Aisgill Moor Cottages, passing the fine waterfall of Hellgill Force.

Lady's Pillar

NINE STANDARDS

Most fellwalkers remember clearly the summit details of the mountains and hills they climb: the highest cairns are pinnacles of achievement, the crowning moment of expeditions, the ultimate reward. When fellwalking becomes a passion as it has been for me and many others, the summits are regarded as old friends and memories are refreshed on each visit. In my case, and I am sure I am not alone in this, I can picture in my mind's eye every summit I have reached in a long life without confusion of identity. But to many occasional and less enthusiastic walkers all mountain tops look very much alike, the characteristics are not ingrained in memory and are soon forgotten. There is one felltop, however, that everybody who has been there will remember vividly ever after. This is Nine Standards.

Nine Standards is the name given to a line of ancient piles of stones, nine in all, built into large cairns by forgotten men centuries ago and adding great distinction to a bleak moorland plateau. Their origins are obscure. They are mentioned by name on eighteenth-century maps and referred to in Sir Walter Scott's *The Bridal of Triermain*; they are often supposed to mark the county boundary, which they do not, and the most popular theory is that they were erected at the time of the Border raids to delude Scots advancing up the Eden valley, from which they are conspicuously in view, into the belief that an English army was encamped there.

The nine cairns stand in wilderness country without habitations or shelter, in pathless terrain hostile to easy progress. Although there are pockets of limestone around, the fell is of underlying gritstone with the usual attendant peat hags and marshy ground. The walking is rough. But it should be undertaken: there is no other place like Nine Standards.

The ascent is usually made from the charming village of Hartley, near Kirkby Stephen, where a rising road passing the huge Hartley Quarry is available for cars to a point where a cart track branches off and heads into the hills. This formerly served some coal pits, long abandoned, which are reached after two further miles. Here the track ends and the rough and pathless western slope of Nine Standards Rigg directly ahead must be tackled, aiming left to score a bull's-eye by arriving exactly at the nine cairns.

A shorter and easier route of ascent may be made from Birkdale Summit, the top of the B6270 road linking Kirkby Stephen and Keld, by making the car do most of the climbing; the ribbon of tarmac spirals up to almost 1700 feet where there is parking space. A walk across the moor to the north from this point soon arrives at an area of limestone pierced by the many shafts of Tailbrigg Pots. Beyond here, by continuing north, a wall surrounding the valley of

Tailbrigg Pots

Dukerdale (which carries Rigg Beck, a haunt of botanists) is rounded and the cart track coming up from Hartley is joined near the coal pits at the base of the final slope.

The nine cairns stand on the northern rim of the broad ridge named Nine Standards Rigg and command an uninterrupted and comprehensive view of many miles of the valley of the Eden. To the north are the giants of the Pennines and eastwards are interminable rolling moors divided by the loneliest and least-known of the Yorkshire Dales, the wild recess of Whitsundale. The ridge is stony but easily followed south to its highest point, at 2170 feet, indicated by an Ordnance column. A descent of the western slope at this point returns the walker to the old coal pits from which the routes of ascent thus far can be retraced.

Arrival on Nine Standards Rigg is a joyous occasion for Coast to Coast walkers from the Irish Sea to the North Sea, and is the greatest milestone on the long journey. From here onwards, all streams drain in the direction of the marching feet: eastwards to the ultimate destination which induces a feeling of optimism that from now on all will be downhill and easy – sadly, a delusion. But it is a good moment.

Nine Standards

Wain Wath Force

KELD

Keld is a Norse word meaning 'a spring' and the first settlers here could not have chosen a more appropriate name for there is always the sound of water; the little cluster of stone buildings occupies a headland thrust into the turbulent cataracts of the Swale, in infancy Yorkshire's most exuberant river.

Keld gives the impression of a place apart, unaffected by the happenings of the world outside; an insular community, sturdily independent and concerned only with its own affairs. Doorways and walls and even the chapel belfry are adorned with dates and inscriptions relating not to national events and national heroes but to local 'statesmen' of past generations. Keld has changed little. There is still the same straggle of dwellings fronting the street down to the river, all mellowed with antiquity; there is still the same atmosphere of undisturbed tranquillity. Keld is the last outpost of civilisation in Swaledale, secluded in a hollow of the hills; it is an oasis of cultivated fields enclosed by stone walls, each with its barn, in a surround of barren and inhospitable moorlands. Horses and carts were the only means of transport until an infrequent bus service came up the valley to add a further lifeline.

But no longer is there the old feeling of isolation. The advent of the car and the discovery of Keld by motorists have lessened the remoteness and loneliness of the village and recently it has become a crossroads of long-distance walkers, the Pennine Way and the Coast to Coast Walk meeting briefly at a footbridge over the river. There is a Youth Hostel and a few cottages provide overnight accommodation; once there was an inn, the Cathole, but now a fading memory.

The supreme joy of Keld is the river, hurrying in a mad rush from its desolate beginnings as it thrashes through a channel it has carved in the limestone in a series of cascades and waterfalls. This is a lovely setting amongst native trees.

A day spent exploring the environs of Keld is a day to remember.

A visitor to Keld does not have to be a long-distance walker to enjoy the scenic delights of the environs. Short rambles, mostly along the riverside, provide pleasure in surroundings of rare beauty. Boots are advisable and cameras are essential for those who like to preserve their memories in photographs. Four walks in particular deserve mention.

1: Wain Wath Force is alongside the Birkdale road a short mile out of the village and can be viewed by motorists without leaving their cars. But if a little exercise is desired, first cross the bridge on the Tan Hill road and follow a path upriver along the edge of cliffs and descend to another bridge to regain the Birkdale road, returning along it past the Force.

2: Another fine sight is Catrake Force, quickly reached from the cottages on the left at the bottom of the street in Keld. In spate, this is the most spectacular of the waterfalls, and its thunderous roar can be heard from afar.

3: A rough lane goes downriver from the bottom end of the street in Keld and this soon develops into a lovely path amongst trees from which Kisdon Force is reached by a short detour. Here the river is confined in a narrow channel, displaying a final turbulence before flowing more sedately through the fields and meadows of Swaledale.

Catrake Force

4: From the lane leading to Kisdon Force, a signposted path diverges and comes to a footbridge over the river. Here the two long-distance walks briefly coincide, the footbridge being crossed by thousands of booted and laden pedestrians every year. On the far bank, where a tributary of the Swale forms the waterfall of East Gill Force, a short climb arrives at a lane and here the two routes part company, never again to meet: Pennine Wayfarers turn left for Tan Hill, and Coast to Coasters turn right across a bridge to follow the lane eastwards high above the gorge of the Swale to reach Crackpot Hall.

Crackpot Hall is a sad ruin in a beautiful location. Now bereft of roofs and windows, its sightless eyes command a superb view of the Swale far below. Mining activity nearby was the cause of its abandonment in the 1950s, when evidences of subsidence became apparent. Today it is in a state of total decay, only the delightful prospect over the river remaining to tell of its former glory. The mines have long been closed but a relic survives in a blacksmith's forge behind the crumbled walls.

The walk may be continued beyond the ruins to Swinner Gill where a track leads upstream to the site of the Swinnergill Lead Mine, a scene of industrial devastation, a scarred landscape that nature has been unable to heal. There is very little pretty here, only the limestone ravine of Swinnergill Kirk being worthy of the camera. It is, however, a fascinating area to explore, bridges, culverts, mine levels and a smelting mill remaining to be seen after a century of abandonment and neglect.

The return to Keld must be made the same way; there is no alternative.

The ruins of Crackpot Hall 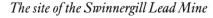 *The site of the Swinnergill Lead Mine*

THE BUTTERTUBS

A remarkable feature, well known to travellers in the Yorkshire Dales and a compulsive halt for all who pass by, is the group of potholes on both sides of the road linking Wensleydale and Swaledale between Hawes and Thwaite. So obvious are these vertical shafts and so compelling an attraction that it is usual on a fine day to find a line of cars parked along the roadside and people of all ages timidly visiting each one to peer into the depths. The holes are unfenced but their dangers are sufficiently apparent to deter too adventurous an inspection.

These potholes, occurring unexpectedly in an area of bare moorland, are known as the Buttertubs and are of varying depths up to 80 feet. The largest hole, immediately alongside the road, admits a small stream and one can hear the sound of subterranean waters but, unusually, there are no underground passages connecting the series. The name derives from their similar appearance, more imagined than real, to the buttertubs formerly in common use among the farming communities in the district.

The Buttertubs

HARDRAW FORCE

Hardraw, as every good Yorkshireman knows, is a hamlet on a byroad two miles from Hawes in Wensleydale. Although insignificant on the map, it has long been a magnet drawing folk from the Dales on repeated visits; latterly there has been a growing influx of tourists and walkers from outside the county to see the magnificent waterfall of Hardraw Force. In earlier days, a secondary attraction brought the crowds: brass band concerts and contests regularly took place on a green sward at the entrance to the glen leading to the waterfall, the acoustics being excellent. Rough terraces of seats were fashioned to serve as an auditorium. These happy festivities still occasionally take place.

Unchanged, however, are the environs of the great waterfall at the head of the valley, a scene of awesome natural grandeur where, in a surround of towering limestone cliffs, Hardraw Beck plunges over the lip of a crag in a graceful unbroken leap of a hundred feet. The approach is exciting and when the fall is suddenly revealed around a bend in the path, the effect is electrifying, a shock to the senses. No matter how often seen before, memories of earlier visits never match the reality of the superb setting, the stark rocks being relieved by a fringe of trees. A mild adventure is offered: the base of the crag is undercut, permitting walkers to pass behind the curtain of falling water.

The Green Dragon Inn at Hardraw

Hardraw Force is the highest surface waterfall in the country (although exceeded in height by a few underground streams descending into potholes, Fell Beck in Gaping Gill being a notable example) and the most beautiful. Access to the valley is gained through the doorway of the Green Dragon Inn on payment of a small admission charge for the upkeep of the path. Money was never better spent. I consider Hardraw Force to be the most impressive natural feature in the north.

In less sophisticated days earlier this century, wanderers in the Dales were often amused by coming across little quirks of unspoken and primitive humour. The notice on a men's urinal at the back of the inn at Hardraw simply announced 'Beer Depository'. At Hubberholme, in the heart of sheep farming country, the two doors of the public lavatories were labelled not 'Ladies' and 'Gentlemen' but 'Yows' and 'Tups'. Am I wrong in thinking that the old days, if not the best, were the most enjoyable?

Opposite Hardraw Force

Cotter Force

COTTER FORCE

Three miles out of Hawes on the Sedbergh road, a signposted footpath leads through pleasant fields to Cotter Force, a lovely waterfall descending in steps and embowered in trees, a scene perfectly posed for the camera. The stream, on its way to join the River Ure, has its origins on Abbotside Common and passes through the small hidden village of Cotterdale, a community unseen and unsuspected from the main road, the only access to it branching off as a gated strip of tarmac. Here the limestone of the Force gives way to peat moorlands pierced by disused coal pits, abandoned long ago but temporarily revived by the villagers during the coal strike of 1926.

GARSDALE AND GRISEDALE

Running east from Sedbergh to link with Wensleydale is the lovely unspoilt valley of Garsdale, native trees and lush pastures softening the harshness of the confining heights of Baugh Fell and Rise Hill. The valley is drained by the Clough River (unusually so named, this being the only example I can think of where the word 'River' follows the name instead of preceding it). Naked limestone is a feature of the river bed and there are caves in the bank below Danny Bridge in its lower reaches before joining the River Rawthey just before Sedbergh.

Two byroads rise from Garsdale and join to enter the upland side-valley of Grisedale. This is a remote and unfrequented hollow in the hills threaded by a narrow strip of tarmac with the deterrent of many gates. Grisedale once housed a busy farming community but economic necessity after the war caused a sad exodus and the abandonment of farmhouses and buildings. The blight that fell upon the valley was well illustrated in a television documentary 'The Valley That Died'. Now some life has returned, those dwellings that did not fall into ruin having been adopted as holiday homes; even the forsaken chapel has been converted into a residence. But Grisedale remains a sad place.

The name Grisedale, meaning 'the valley of the pigs' is consistently spelt wrongly as Grisdale by the Ordnance Survey.

AYSGARTH FALLS

Aysgarth is a village astride the main road through Wensleydale, and the proud guardian of a spectacular section of the River Ure. It here plunges for half a mile over massive limestone steps in a wide channel flanked by trees: a beautiful sight, always impressive and, in times of spate, awesome. Aysgarth Falls are a great natural attraction, tending to be rather too over-populated at weekends and during the holidays for the comfort of those who prefer to appreciate the wonderful scene without disturbance.

GOD'S BRIDGE, STAINMORE

There are many natural rock bridges over streams in the limestone districts of the Dales, formed by the erosive action of running water. The best example is God's Bridge at Stainmore which spans the River Greta and carries a track now adapted as part of the Pennine Way. Downriver, two insignificant openings on the north bank admit to half a mile of underground passages: these are subject to flooding and should not be entered by other than experienced cavers.

The author on God's Bridge, Stainmore

2 DENTDALE

DENTDALE IS A shy and sequestered valley, not advertising its many and varied charms nor seeking publicity. There are no garish signboards promising services and supplies, no welcoming notices and it is not readily located by strangers without a map. Remote from motorways and dual carriageways and the usual routes of tourists, the valley is hidden in a deep fold of the hills and has remained a sanctuary of rural peace unspoilt and unscathed by modern developments. Shyness in this instance has proved a virtue and its resulting insularity and independence a blessing. Dentdale is special.

The main focus of attention for travellers who do find their way into this concealed paradise is the quaint huddle of buildings ranged along the cobbled streets of Dent Town, a Mecca in miniature to which all steps and wheels lead. Dent is a throwback to medieval times bypassed by modern progress, an anachronism that has survived the passing years. Little has changed here, although the upper galleries of the terraced cottages that overhung the narrow streets and were no hazard in the days of horses and carts have succumbed to the needs of larger traffic. The atmosphere of the little town is that of an age long gone and is best appreciated in late evening when the daily influx of sightseers has departed; then, in silence, a visitor feels an intruder in a very private community in a fairy-tale setting unrelated to reality.

In the old days before the distracting influences of radio and television, the fixed routine of the adult inhabitants after the day's work was done was to settle down for an evening's knitting, a craft both men and women practised assiduously, on the outside galleries in summer and by candlelight in front of a peat fire in winter. So addicted were they to this practice, which relieved their frugal existence by exporting their products to the more populous dales, that they earned a reputation as 'the terrible knitters of Dent': terrible not because their handiwork was slipshod but because of their complete dedication to the craft.

The humble cottages are presided over by the tower of the venerable church of St Andrew, founded in the twelfth century but rebuilt and restored since with some sacrifice of its earlier features. Near the entrance to the churchyard, on the main street a massive block of Shap granite, adapted as a drinking fountain, is a memorial to Dent's most renowned son, Adam Sedgwick. A pupil of Dent Grammar School, Sedgwick became one of the founders of the science of geology and had a long career as Professor of Geology at Cambridge University, where he was buried in 1873 at the age of ninety-eight.

Throughout a long history, Dent was the administrative, electoral and scholastic centre of a wide rural district but suffered a slow decline in importance with the founding and subsequent development of a large public school in neighbouring Sedbergh, pronounced Sedber. With the resulting growth there in shopping, commercial and residential facilities, Sedbergh took over the administrative responsibilities of the district in 1863. Local people, however, often speak of Dent Town as a reminder of the days when Dent had the greater status.

Dent Town suffered its gradual loss of status passively and withdrew into its shell, content to look after its own affairs exclusively and be bypassed by a changing world. It was a close-knit community with no ambition to expand its interests and activities. Everybody knew everybody else, as had always been the case, and few strangers ever appeared. There were no new settlers, no new buildings. Dent was happy to be left alone.

When I first went to Dent, before the war, I arrived at dusk, hungry and footsore after walking all day. As I entered the cobbled main street, I became aware of a feeling of unease. The little community was shrouded in silence: there was no movement, no sign of life. In the half-light, the tiny cottages seemed unreal, like cardboard cutouts, or the deserted film set of a seventeenth-century village. I was a Gulliver, viewing a strange scene outside my experience. Dent was a ghost town that night. . . . I made my way to a cottage near the church, where I had been told I could expect a night's lodging. I was admitted and accepted. It was a strange evening. The woman busied herself in the kitchen and produced a plate piled high like a cairn with potatoes, and a huge pot of tea, and then resumed her knitting by the fire opposite her husband. There was little conversation: nothing had happened in Dent that day worth the telling, and it was none of their business to ask where I had come from and where I was going. But they were kind: the man roused himself at my request to hammer a protruding nail in my shoe that had caused me discomfort, the woman interrupted her knitting to refill my pot of tea and make sure the meal was to my liking. After supper I was shown to a tiny bedroom overlooking and adjoining the graveyard; so profound was the silence that I felt part of it. I was so physically tired that I slept as soundly as the corpses outside the window but, unlike them, awoke refreshed and went downstairs to a good breakfast. Then I paid the woman the five shillings she asked for her hospitality and went on my way.

In the morning sunlight Dent was no longer a fantasy but a solid and compact cluster of dwellings of a past age. Not until I was out in the open countryside again, reassured by the songs of the birds and the murmur of streams did I feel that I had emerged from a dream and rejoined the familiar twentieth century.

Main Street, Dent

Dentdale

Today Dent is very different. Not in appearance which has changed little, nor in character which remains in essence that of a medieval settlement, but the former strongly individual atmosphere of the place, the aura of bygone days, has been destroyed by the coming of the motor car which increasingly has taken away the privacy of the little town. On summer weekends, chattering crowds of sightseers parade the narrow streets and blaring transistor radios wreck the peace; a parking area to keep vehicles off the cobbles has been enlarged progressively to the dimensions of a football pitch and soon fills to capacity. Dent is so refreshingly different from the city environments of most of the visitors that it would be churlish to deny them this glimpse of a way of life that belongs to history. Their presence augments the local economy, but there are treasures greater than money. I liked Dent better fifty years ago.

Most visitors to Dentdale gravitate to Dent Town and halt there without exploring further and remain unaware of the many other delights to be found in the ten miles of this lovely valley, some man-made and others the work of a bountiful nature. There are hidden recesses, mature native woodlands, a tree-fringed river of great charm and many other surprises – narrow lanes between fragrant hedgerows, pleasant secluded paths and a scattering of isolated and attractive farmsteads, all enclosed by colourful hills and unfrequented by the weekend tourists. The only disturbance to the peace of this natural sanctuary occurred 120 years ago when a spectacular railway was laid at a high level across the head of the valley; this apart, Dentdale today is very much as it was three centuries ago, happily free from modern developments and well content to remain so.

The valley is watered by the River Dee which rises high on Blea Moor and is precocious in infancy, playing hide and seek behind a screen of trees, often disappearing in fissures of its limestone bed and emerging to daylight lower downstream. It sculptures caves in its banks as it falls into a deep ravine, and becomes sedate only in its later stages as it leaves its dale to lose its identity in the River Lune.

The usual approach to Dentdale is from the town of Sedbergh where two side roads signposted Dent join to cross the River Rawthey at Millthrop Bridge. Immediately beyond, a short lane leads up to a long terrace of cottages built to house the workers of the Millthrop woollen mill nearby across the river, and looking rather forlorn and out of place since their source of employment was destroyed by fire many years ago. The main road curves in a wide sweep around the base of Frostrow, a green hill forming a high barrier to the promised land, and enters Dentdale through an avenue of trees. Although unclassified, the road has the luxury of a white centre line, a rarity in the valley. The River Dee is below on the right, concealed by woodlands that once harboured a colony of red deer: access to it by cars is provided by a descending side road to a bridge near a chapel with a corrugated iron roof and a former sawmill in sylvan surroundings. From this point, a single-track lane with many gates may be followed upriver to rejoin the road a mile short of Dent: a journey not recommended to anyone in a hurry. The main road is no less attractive and much quicker, passing the residence of Gate, a Victorian house built in mock Tudor style, and many delectable wayside cottages before crossing the Dee and, after being joined by a road from Barbondale near the ancient settlement of Gawthrop, heads directly into Dent Town.

Dent Town is really no more than a village, although it may not be prudent to say so in the hearing of the residents. If you can resist its obvious appeal, Dent can be quickly entered and left for the further reaches of the valley which, for me, has always held greater interest and excitement. At the Sedgwick memorial, the main street continues ahead and a branch turns right, these rejoining at Cowgill a few miles further on; this branch road will be described on the return journey.

The main road goes on to cross the River Dee at Church Bridge and soon narrows between hedgerows, two signposts indicating footpaths to the river. After passing Cross House and noting its sundial, the road arrives at the sad ruin of Gibb's Hall, once a handsome building with literary associations; it was here that Mary Howitt wrote a novel about Dentdale called *Hope On, Hope Ever*. At this point, there is a first opportunity to park a car. A roadside gate opposite admits to a field sloping down to the river (no path; no right of way so seek permission to visit) where, in a wild and impressive setting, the Dee, here flowing in a deep ravine, leaps in a waterfall into a deep pool beneath a high canopy of trees. This is Hell's Cauldron, a scenic gem.

The ruins of Gibb's Hall

Hell's Cauldron

At Hell's Cauldron, an opening at the base of the cliff alongside is one of a series of cave entrances piercing the banks of the ravine for half a mile upriver. This is the most spectacular section of the Dee, its steep confining walls fringed by dense woodlands and its rocky bed much too rough for the passage of walkers not addicted to hard labour and who have respect for their clothes. This is the exclusive preserve of the cave explorer who cares less for personal discomfort. Some of these riverbank cave entrances are submerged when the river is in spate making their underground passages subject to sudden flooding. A feature of this section is a stream issuing from Hackergill Cave on the south bank, but this, along with the other wonders of the river hereabouts, must be regarded as out of bounds by the prudent pedestrian. The Dee here is for intrepid cavemen only.

But, at the head of the ravine, a visit may, and should, be made to the waterfall of Ibbeth Peril, a twin to Hell's Cauldron – the names themselves provoke excitement! Ibbeth Peril has secrets it discloses only to brave men but its sylvan surroundings can be enjoyed by all.

Ibbeth Peril is most easily visited by continuing along the road from Gibb's Hall until the dense screen of trees on the right ends at a large open space used by the highway authority for the storage of grit; here is accommodation for several cars. A fingerpost points to a short path descending amongst trees to a footbridge over the river, flowing erratically on and under its limestone bed. The waterfall, however, is a hundred yards downriver and is best reached by walking back along the road for fifty yards to the end of a wall, where a step down in the undergrowth discloses a good path high on the river bank above a deep gorge, the waterfall soon being seen through a canopy of foliage. By proceeding a little further, a scrambling descent to the river bed may be made. The environs of the waterfall are pleasant enough and there is no suspicion of the Peril's dark secret unless a small opening under the overhang of the cliff alongside is noticed: this insignificant hole admits to the largest cave system in the valley, underground passages extending for more than half a mile below and far beyond the road in a succession of tight crawls and large caverns. In flood conditions, the entrance is submerged; in any weather, this is certainly not an adventure for anyone not experienced in the terrors and hazards of subterranean exploration.

Ibbeth Peril

After viewing Ibbeth Peril, visitors who are subject to claustrophobia, and possibly others who are not, will be relieved to escape from its gloomy shroud of trees and continue their journey up the valley in a more open environment with the Dee now alongside the road, its limestone bed bleached a pristine white where the water elects to flow beneath the surface. The branch road from Dent joins in at a bridge and the hamlet of Cowgill, once a parish in its own right, is immediately beyond: here is a church built in 1873, a converted school, the pleasant residence and gardens of Cowgill Grange and an isolated terrace of cottages. A little further on, the small compact settlement of Lea Yeat (Gate) is reached, its tranquillity disturbed only in the 1870s when the railway was being constructed across the hillside above. A side road leaves here and climbs steeply to Dent Station, four long miles from the town it was intended to serve, and continues at a high level before descending to Garsdale Head. This road, known as the Coal Road because it was used for the transport of coal from long-abandoned pits, discloses an aerial view of the hidden valley of Grisedale across the gulf of Garsdale.

At Lea Yeat, the river is crossed and accompanies the road along the valley, which now trends south. After passing the welcome but rather unexpected Sportsman's Inn, the river is re-crossed at Stone House Bridge, one of the few places on this narrow highway where there is space to park a few cars. Across the bridge a no-through-road branches off to Stone House Farm and discloses ahead the massive Artengill Viaduct, eleven lofty arches spanning a hollow in the skyline in a remarkable feat of railway engineering. A track continues up to the viaduct and the detour is worth the effort to see and admire the impressive

Artengill Viaduct

structure at close range. Note in particular the embossed imprints of fossils in the huge blocks of stone which form the base of the piers of the arches.

Stone House is the silent grave of an active industry that died at the turn of the present century. In Victorian times there was a flourishing 'marble' works here, of which only the site remains; it engaged in the cutting, dressing and polishing of dark grey limestone won from nearby quarries to produce an appearance of marble, but which was made even more attractive by the presence of fossil patterns in the stone. Dent marble was in demand for fireplace surrounds and ornamental and decorative purposes but the trade lapsed and succumbed, like the lead mines of Swaledale, when cheaper foreign imports became available.

Resuming the journey from Stone House Bridge, the road now starts a long climb to its summit, rising gently at first and with the Dee an inseparable companion alongside. It passes a tearoom and a craft shop that confirm the emancipation of the valley from the pre-car days when few travellers came this way. A small bridge gives access to a Youth Hostel, adapted from a private residence, with extensive outbuildings and a row of cottages, an idyllic complex that patrons must be loth to leave. The road steepens to reach and pass alongside Dent Head Viaduct, the tremendous arched buttresses soaring high above with dramatic effect, the whole a remarkable tribute to the skill of the Victorian railway engineers. There is space to halt a car here of which, on a first visit, advantage should be taken to survey the scenic masterpiece presented by the sturdy elegance and symmetrical beauty of the viaduct. Its near presence is rather overpowering and intimidating yet it is softened by the verdant greenery around its base. There is easy access to the foot of one of the buttresses where the mammoth task of construction is better appreciated and the industry and enterprise of the builders more fully admired: these craftsmen of a past age here erected a work of art that has become their own memorial and puts to shame the undistinguished concrete structures favoured by the builders of today, builders who have the benefits of modern technology yet seem too often prepared to sacrifice character to utility. Just beyond, spanning a feeder of the Dee as it passes under the viaduct, is an ancient packhorse bridge, happily preserved but appearing incongruously insignificant below the mighty railway arches. It indicates the route of travellers centuries earlier.

Packhorse bridge, Dent Head

Dent Head Viaduct

The road bypasses the viaduct, preferring to cross under the railway at a more orthodox bridge a short distance further on, after which it climbs steadily in a barren landscape to the grassy tableland of Newby Head Moss at an elevation of almost 1400 feet. This is the end of Dentdale, a fact signalled by a roadside sign announcing entry into the county of North Yorkshire. This is the county boundary, new since a revision in 1974 when the valleys of Garsdale and Dentdale, hitherto giving allegiance to Yorkshire, were decreed to be henceforth attached to the new county of Cumbria. This made geographical sense: both valleys drain west to the River Lune and the Irish Sea and are separated from the rest of Yorkshire by the barrier of the Pennines; nevertheless, the breaking of traditional ties was not to the liking of all the inhabitants. Cumbria has not yet acknowledged the new boundary by a sign.

A short distance further on, the road ends at the Hawes—Ingleton highway where cars can make a U-turn for the return to Dentdale.

The descent into Dentdale from Newby Head is even more stimulating than the outward journey, new aspects of the valley being revealed when seen in the reverse direction, with wider and more distant landscapes coming into view.

Beyond the last buildings of Cowgill, a bridge over the river admits to the branch road that gives an alternative return to Dent Town. This is very narrow, more akin to a country lane, with few passing places, but is relatively traffic free. The roads in this upper part of the valley were designed in medieval times for the occasional passage of horses and carts and have never been brought to modern standards by straightening and widening and it is to be hoped that they never will be. Dentdale is a typical sixteenth-century English countryside, peaceful, undisturbed and all the sweeter for its absence of fast roads and speeding motorists. An advantage of this slender branch byway, which runs at a higher level than the main road, is the splendid panorama it affords of the encircling hills: across the valley the distant double-topped Frostrow merges in the long whaleback skyline of Rise Hill; at the head is Great Knoutberry Hill carrying the railway; rising to the left are the lower slopes of Whernside, succeeded by Great Coum beyond the gap of Deepdale, and finally Middleton Fell closes the horizon. Only to the west where the Dee has carved its channel is there an escape from Dentdale without climbing.

An imposing gateway on the left of the road is the entrance to the drive of Whernside Manor, the largest residence in the valley, with its attendant home farm and cottages. For many years it was a centre for cave exploration but was recently acquired by the Royal Signals for adventure and training.

A short distance further on at the foot of the side-valley of Deepdale and snugly sheltered by a background of trees, is the Methodist Chapel of Deepdale, a survivor amongst the many Methodist chapels in the district that have ceased to provide services and been sold. The road passes by the chapel and is soon joined on the left by a road coming from Ingleton and this offers an opportunity for a brief detour to see Deepdale. And Deepdale is too good to miss.

From the junction, the Ingleton road climbs steadily to traverse a wooded hillside where the pastoral beauty of Deepdale is revealed below. A few scattered farmsteads and the beck, a main tributary of the Dee, backed by the rising slopes of Whernside, make a picture of rural tranquillity. After two miles, and near the limits of cultivation, the roadside waterfall of Lockin Garth appears suddenly on the right.

Whernside Manor

Above *Path from Flinter Gill*

Below *Approach to Dent from the south*

There is space at the waterfall for parking or a picnic, and here cars must be turned for the journey back to Dent. Travellers on foot, however, may continue along the road to its barren summit, and return to Dent on an ancient highway that joins here on the right. This track offers a splendid high-level walk free of traffic; it finally descends to Dent by way of Flinter Gill after passing below a hilltop crowned by a group of old cairns known as Megger Stones.

Motorists, denied this exhilarating walk, must return to Dent on wheels, reaching the village a mile from the junction at the foot of Deepdale.

Through Dent on the road to Sedbergh, a signpost to Gawthrop is an invitation to an attractive alternative route to the Lune Valley by way of Barbondale, next to be described.

3 BARBONDALE AND EASE GILL

THE VALLEY OF THE River Lune between Sedbergh and Kirkby Lonsdale is bounded on the east by a lofty range of hills forming a continuous high skyline broken only at one point where a pronounced gap indicates the narrow cutting of Barbondale, carrying a lonely road over a low watershed to Dentdale. This solitary traffic link, once unfrequented, has now been discovered by motorists who seek a respite from the popular tourist routes.

The Lune is accompanied by the A683, from which a byroad, announced as a main road by an antiquity at the junction, leads into the pleasant village of Barbon. This quiet community, made even quieter by the closing of its railway station on a dismantled branch line that linked the Leeds—Lancaster railway with the main line from Euston, springs to animated life on two days every year. This is when it suffers (or enjoys?) an invasion of cars and motor cycles on hill climbs promoted by the Westmorland Motor Club up the spiralling drive to Barbon Manor. The mansion is perched high above the valley and has a commanding view; it was the home, until his death, of Roger Fulford, a Royal historian of national repute.

Barbon village street

Through the village, the road into Barbondale rises sharply before contouring for a level mile along the side of Barbon Low Fell, new plantings of conifers permitting only glimpses of Barbon Manor high on the left. After crossing Blindbeck Bridge, which spans a tributary of Barbon Beck, the main stream draining the valley, a large open space alongside the road invites a halt. Looking up the hillside to the north from this point, the splendid cairn of Josse Pike can be seen prominently. The cairn was erected in the 1870s by the local gamekeeper and named after him: it stands twelve feet high with an interior providing shelter, and occupies a vantage point from which Josse could survey the whole of his domain. From the open space, the road continues straight as an arrow with Barbon Beck now alongside, the narrow strip of tarmac crossing a watershed and descending to Gawthrop after four lonely miles without habitations; Dent Town is then reached one mile further on.

Barbondale

Above *Blindbeck Bridge*

Below *Aygill Caverns*

There is little surface evidence of limestone in Barbondale. Attention will mainly be directed to the towering mass of Middleton Fell on the west side of the valley, very steep slopes ruling out any thought of ascent; Barbon High Fell, rising on the east, is also uninviting although easier of access. Between these confining heights Barbon Beck pursues an uneventful course. In fact, the valley appears devoid of interesting features. Yet cave explorers, always indefatigable in their search for holes in the ground, have discovered several apertures in the beds of the streams coming down from Barbon High Fell, many of them admitting to underground passages and caves attained only by arduous effort. Others of less consequence are found in the upper reaches of Barbon Beck, but the most prolific concentration of entrances to subterranea lies upstream of Blindbeck Bridge.

From the roadside a short distance west of Blindbeck Bridge, a cart track branches off at a tangent and climbs easily to the shallow depression between Barbon Low Fell and Barbon High Fell, having the stream (named as Aygill by the Ordnance Survey and as Barkin Gill by the caving fraternity) away on the left. Nothing is seen from the track to suggest the exciting underworld here apart from the covered shaft of Barbon Pot nearby: this deep hole is used as a grave for dead sheep, but their bones and rotting carcases have not deterred enthusiastic cavers from exploring the passages and caverns extending from the gloomy depths.

As the track crosses the depression on its way to Bullpot Farm and the wonderland of Ease Gill, there are no indications that below the surface at this point is the extensive and intricate network of Aygill Caverns.

Travellers on foot in Barbondale can walk to Bullpot Farm via the track in fifteen minutes but motorists must suffer for their superiority in transport by making a necessary ten-mile detour to reach that desolate but desirable objective by road. Desirable, that is, only to seekers after adventure; to the majority of others it is the last place on earth deserving a visit. Cars must go back to the A683 beyond Barbon and that road followed south to the next village of Casterton, which has a school founded for the daughters of clergy and made famous by its association with the Brontë sisters. At a roadside cottage at the end of the village (a former toll bar), a narrow lane turns off the main road to the left and continues beyond a crossroads and the old railway track to start a long climb on the side of Casterton Fell and ultimately come to an end at Bullpot Farm. In the final stages of this journey, Ease Gill can be seen half a mile down the slope on the right.

Bullpot Farm

Farming days at Bullpot are also at an end. Activity here is no longer centred on the surface of the land but on the underworld beneath. For enthusiastic cave explorers, it is a second home.

From high ground in the vicinity of the farm, there is a wide prospect of rolling moorlands backed by Gragareth across the shallow trench of Ease Gill: it is a desolate landscape, a wilderness devoid of trees and habitations and without any promise of beauty. Most urban visitors will flee the scene and never return. But appearances deceive. This vast expanse of grass and heather is a cover concealing a realm of magic and mystery, where since the beginning of time nature has been at work slowly evolving an intricate subterranean labyrinth of caverns, grottoes and canals carved in beautiful designs by the agency of running water.

This hidden wonderland, sculptured in darkness absolute, remained unseen and unsuspected through the ages until the present century when men first ventured into rifts in the ground and beheld in the light of torches an amazing display of sculptured limestone in patterns both incredibly delicate and massive, a living museum of art in many forms. Exploration intensified in the years that followed. Alternative entrances into the black depths were found, new discoveries made and secrets revealed, passages were penetrated to their furthest limits, links were established between them until finally all mysteries were solved. Now the whole complex underground system is interlocked and related, and meticulously mapped.

The wonders of Ease Gill are available only to a privileged few intrepid explorers. Ordinary mortals walking hereabouts will never know the delights of the fairyland below them.

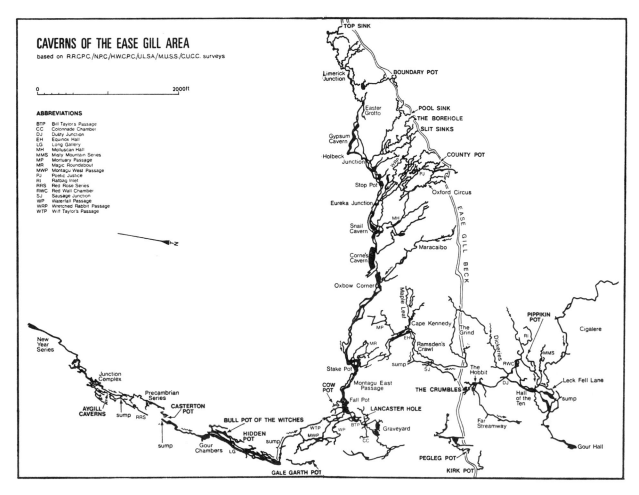

CAVERNS OF THE EASE GILL AREA
based on R.R.C.P.C./N.P.C./H.W.C.P.C./U.L.S.A./M.U.S.S./C.U.C.C. surveys

0   2000ft

ABBREVIATIONS

BTP   Bill Taylors Passage
CC   Colonnade Chamber
DJ   Dusty Junction
EH   Equinox Hall
LG   Long Gallery
MH   Molluscan Hall
MMS   Misty Mountain Series
MP   Mortuary Passage
MR   Magic Roundabout
MWP   Montagu West Passage
PJ   Poetic Justice
RI   Ratbag Inlet
RRS   Red Rose Series
RWC   Red Wall Chamber
SJ   Sausage Junction
WP   Waterfall Passage
WRP   Wretched Rabbit Passage
WTP   Wilf Taylor's Passage

From Northern Caves (Volume 4) © *Dalesman Publishing Co. Ltd.*

Ordinary mortals, however, can visit the area overland by a two-mile circular walk from Bullpot Farm that will give them a hint – but not more than a hint – of the marvels beneath their feet and an appreciation of the bravery of the adventurers who dare to descend from the safety and assurance of daylight into a nether world of total and perpetual blackness. Boots are the only sensible footgear for this expedition, which in places traverses rough and rocky ground.

The lane going east from the farm should be reserved for the return journey and the track heading south to Ease Gill preferred. Within two minutes, a gaping chasm amongst trees opens alongside the track.

This is Bull Pot of the Witches.

Bull Pot of the Witches

Visitors of timid disposition will view Bull Pot of the Witches with apprehension. This fearful hole, scene of a number of fatalities, is 175 feet deep, and from its murky depths, into which a stream cascades, underground passages radiate to form part of the ramifications of the Ease Gill Caverns. There are no witches but they can be imagined. A few paces away, on the opposite side of the track, is Hidden Pot. This is a typical shakehole, caused by a subsidence or collapse of the rocks below. Hidden Pot is succeeded by Gale Garth Pot, and when a wall comes in on the left, a detour along its south side is recommended to the point where it turns northwards.

Looking over the wall corner, the crater of Cow Pot is revealed and should be left severely alone; instead, turn south to a cluster of boulders around an iron manhole cover set in the ground. This place, of no apparent significance, is a vital key admitting to the vast underworld of Ease Gill Caverns. The manhole lid conceals a vertical shaft 110 feet deep. This is Lancaster Hole.

It was discovered by chance. A Lancaster man resting nearby noticed a patch of grass waving agitatedly although the day was calm, and on investigation was aware of a strong draught of air coming up from the ground below. He cleared away the grass and disclosed a narrow opening descending into the darkness. Subsequent excited exploration led to amazing revelations: the shaft was descended and found to enter a network of communicating

Lancaster Pot

chambers and passages hitherto uncharted and displaying a rich array of beautiful limestone carvings. There are today, under the square mile south and east of Bullpot Farm, twenty miles of linked subterranean passages. The Ease Gill cave network is the largest in England.

Returning to the track, the gradual descent is continued, passing a solitary barn, to the limestone bed of Ease Gill Beck. The walk goes upstream, but a short detour to the right should be made to enter the impressive ravine of Easegill Kirk where, in a choke of boulders below towering walls, the beck travels underground to a resurgence in daylight at Leck Beck Head. Easegill Kirk has the awesome silence of a deserted graveyard amid the debris of a shattered cathedral. But it should be seen.

Lower Ease Gill Kirk

Cow Dub

Out of the confines of Easegill Kirk, the beck can be followed upstream without difficulty, passing more cave entrances on the south bank and arriving in half a mile at the waterfall of Cow Dub. A rough scramble alongside leads up into the upper reaches of the beck; here is an untidy tumble of boulders fallen from the enclosing heights but there is one gem where, just above the waterfall, the stream slides smoothly over an immense slab of naked limestone. A decrepit footbridge crosses to the north bank.

Ease Gill Beck rises on the slopes of Crag Hill and after an uneventful early passage meets limestone on the 1200-ft contour, whereupon its flow becomes extremely erratic; its rocky channels are tortured by fissures and crevices that take much of the water. In the short section above Cow Dub, there is a remarkable concentration of cave entrances in both banks, none very obvious, some hidden and needing search. Yet some of these insignificant openings admit to the extensive maze of Ease Gill Caverns.

The best known is County Pot.

The water slide, Ease Gill

County Pot is located among a ruck of boulders 80 yards upstream from the top of the Cow Dub waterfall, its constricted entrance being identified by a manhole cover among many other holes hereabouts on the north bank. This is the usual way into the caverns and remains so despite the later discovery of Lancaster Hole, since the access is easier. It would seem to have taken its name from the county boundary between Cumbria and Lancashire, which coincides with Ease Gill Beck.

Upper Ease Gill above Cow Dub

There is an easy route of return to Bullpot Farm from County Pot. A new path nearby climbs the steep bank and, without further excitement, crosses the moor above to reach the lane entering the farm from the east.

I should point out that nothing in this book should be construed as implying that I am an authority on the caves and potholes I mention. Far from it. I have never descended a pothole, and have ventured with a flashlight only in the caves promised by caving journals to be without danger. My interest has always been in locating the various holes on the surface from descriptions I have read.

My best year for this pursuit was 1948. With a shilling guidebook that was woefully inaccurate in its measurement of distances but was the only one then available, I hunted down all the hundred holes then known (today there are thousands); it was not an easy task because many have concealed entrances, but great fun. Ever since I have had a huge interest in any new discovery and great admiration for those who seek adventure below ground. I prefer daylight to darkness. I would rather go up than down.

4   LECK FELL AND GRAGARETH

MANY PLACES OF INTEREST on and around the Three Peaks can only be reached on foot after many miles of walking over rough ground, but visitors to Leck Fell are favoured by a quiet moorland road that takes them to their objective precisely and, if they travel by car, without effort. When they arrive there, they may well wonder why they have come, for Leck Fell at first sight appears to have no compelling attractions, certainly no obvious ones. It is a barren and featureless wasteland without even a tree to relieve the dreariness of the landscape.

But there is more to it than meets the eye. Leck Fell is as full of holes as a much-used pin cushion but there the similarity ends, some of the holes penetrating the ground to depths of around 400 feet. It is not a place for the faint hearted or those who swoon easily: such are advised to remain in the safety of the car. But active adventurers who are content merely to locate the various holes and inspect them from secure stances on the surface will reap an experience they will long remember.

The road to the fell leaves the A65 at Cowan Bridge, a small village where a tablet on the gable of a former school proudly proclaims that the Brontë sisters were educated there in 1824–25 before the transfer of the school to Casterton. Leck Beck passes under the road nearby from its rising in Easegill Kirk. The narrow road to Leck goes between buildings and immediately assumes a rural character, reaching the little community of Leck after a pleasant mile graced by lovely trees. Leck is quiet and secluded, a place apart from the pulsating world outside and rarely disturbed by strangers. The fell road continues ahead, rising above its wooded surroundings to climb gradually, between walls, to a desolate moorland, colourful only when the heather is in bloom. After three miles and at an altitude of 1200 feet, the walls end at a gateway, and here cars must be parked. Clear of constricting walls, the prospect ahead and around can be surveyed. The ribbon of tarmac goes on to the lonely outpost of Leck Fell House, a speck of civilisation in a wide panorama that has no other sign of life. Mile after mile of undulating uplands extend in sombre silence to distant horizons in anonymous array with no distinguishing landmarks apart from cairns on the nearer Gragareth skyline. It is a primeval wilderness tamed only where men built boundary walls two centuries ago, finding and cutting the stone they needed, feeding and sleeping on the site, and all for a few pence a day. The drystone walls on Leck Fell, Gragareth and elsewhere are memorials to their skill and industry.

From the road, Leck Fell declines in a mile-long slope to Ease Gill and its main concentration of potholes are reached in a ten-minute walk; others, much lower down the slope, form part of the Ease Gill cave system and are too far to be visited if Gragareth is also in the itinerary.

But first in the day's programme must be Lost John's Cave.

Lost John's Cave is found very easily by rounding the end of the wall on the right and walking back alongside for 180 yards to a hollow where a small stream enters a black cavity in a low cliff; a few yards further over a small rise is another less obvious orifice. These are the two entrances to Lost John's Cave, the best known and most extensive underground system in the Leck Fell area; it is highly complex and has passages descending on various levels to a depth of 460 feet.

Clearly this is no place for novices but it is possible for them, if armed with a torch and wearing boots and clothes that don't matter, to go into one hole and emerge from the other, the two entrance passages converging after fifteen yards of stumbling progress. The passage continuing beyond the junction is absolutely out of bounds.

Lost John's Cave: left *The stream entrance*, right *The dry entrance*

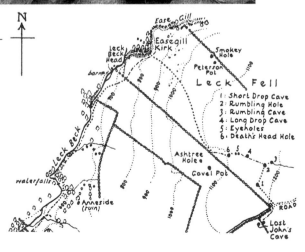

Returning to the car, those shaken by the mild adventure of the visit to Lost John's Cave should get in and await any other members of the party who are inspired to go in search of other holes on Leck Fell.

A wall goes down from the road straight as a die to Ease Gill and a walk alongside leads in a few minutes to a small hole in the ground that opens into lengthy passages below: this is Short Drop Cave. A little distance further across the moor to the north-east, a stream disappears into Rumbling Beck Cave which, followed overland, soon brings into close view the fearful abyss of Rumbling Hole.

Above *Rumbling Hole*
Below *Death's Head Hole*

Rumbling Hole graphically demonstrates the danger of walking on Leck Fell after dark. It is an evil slit, a place fit for a horror film. It is fortunately fenced to deter a too-close inspection of its vertical shaft that descends 390 feet into the bowels of the earth, admitting, just below the surface, the stream issuing from Rumbling Cave as a waterfall. Strange noises in the nether regions have given this awesome place its name.

Continuing in the same direction, Long Drop Cave may be seen at the base of a low cliff, and this is succeeded by a series of minor potholes known as the Eyeholes which seem almost friendly by comparison.

Most of the potholes and caves on Leck Fell and elsewhere occur in hollows and shallow valleys and are revealed only after a search, but the next great chasm in the line of march is identified by a fence and cannot be missed. This is Death's Head Hole, the name itself enough to cause a shudder. This is a twin in terror to Rumbling Hole. Timid observers will marvel at the bravery of the men who dare descend into these black pits for enjoyment and adventure: their reward is a visit to a fantastic nether world the rest of us will never see.

Death's Head Hole concludes the recommended foray on Leck Fell and the nearby boundary wall can be followed up to the road. Other explorers with more time available can go down the slope to Ease Gill and there locate Leck Beck Head; here all the streams that disappear underground on Leck Fell join those from Ease Gill in a return to daylight.

Back at the car a decision must be made: whether or not to climb Gragareth. It is not far in distance but is a tough assignment, pathless, very rough underfoot with no mercy for tired legs. Those members of the party who do not feel inclined can perform a service for those who do by returning in the car to Leck and there taking a side road past Leck Church to the village of Ireby; here they can await the arrival of their more resolute companions.

Above *The Three Men of Gragareth*

Below *The summit of Gragareth*

Gragareth looms large ahead and to the right. It is best reached by continuing along the road, now unenclosed, until near Leck Fell House when a steep scramble up the hillside ends in the company of the three massive cairns that will have plagued the curiosity since they first came in sight earlier. These ancient piles of stones, long known as the Three Men of Gragareth, have an origin beyond the memory of man: they stand side by side, mute sentinels overlooking a vast panorama that has never changed and never will.

The domain guarded by the Three Men is, however, unworthy of such distinguished surveillance. A long half-mile to the east, across a rising plateau, is the summit of Gragareth and it is reached only after a stumbling progress through untamed and unfriendly vegetation. Nobody has ever taken the trouble to build a cairn on the bare top but the Ordnance surveyors have erected a triangulation column to mark the highest point at 2058 feet. A saving grace is the stone wall nearby that adorns the eight-mile ridge between Dent and Ireby, a monumental task undertaken by rough men long before the coming of trade unions. Today the wall serves as a safe guide back to civilisation in mist or unkind weather and lost souls on Gragareth have good reason to be grateful for its existence.

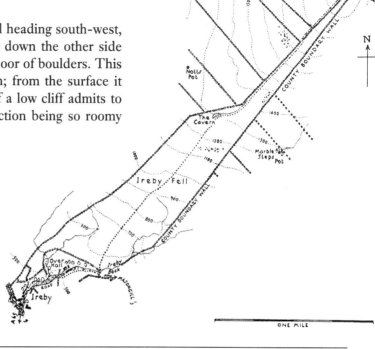

To reach Ireby, descend alongside the wall heading south-west, crossing it where convenient and continuing down the other side until confronted by a large shakehole with a floor of boulders. This is named on Ordnance maps as The Cavern; from the surface it promises little, but an opening at the base of a low cliff admits to miles of subterranean passages, one long section being so roomy that it has earned the name of Duke Street.

Continuing down the slope, the trees and cottages of Ireby beckon a welcome and here, if all has gone according to plan, should be a waiting car, its occupants probably in a bad temper after a five-hour vigil. Ireby is very pleasant, with a stream running alongside its only street, and the possibility of afternoon tea, but its attractions are not sufficient to engage attention for half a day.

Ireby

Gragareth is not hostile everywhere. At mid-height along its eastern flank is an easy terrace above a belt of limestone traversed by a cart track known as the Turbary Road (turbary being a place where peat is dug), giving an exhilarating walk with open views across the valley of Kingsdale to Whernside; there is much of interest to see along the route with three spectacular highlights. The most convenient place to start the walk is the small secluded settlement of Masongill, reached by a signposted byroad from the A65 two miles west of Ingleton.

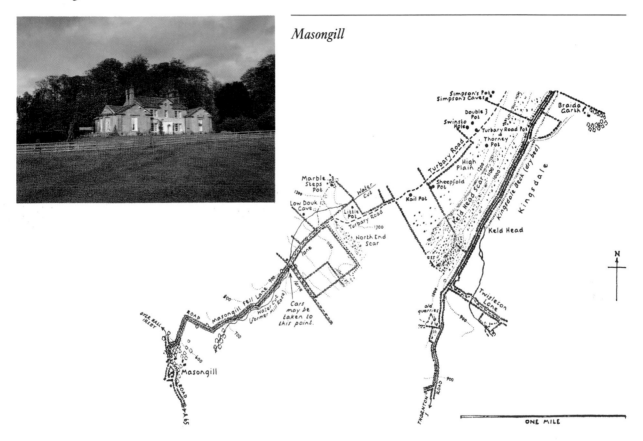

Masongill

Masongill, within sound of the busy A65 yet remote from it, is a peaceful oasis undisturbed by tourists who, in the absence of any welcoming invitations to visit, speed past for other destinations. Mature trees make this an attractive place but there is no offer of hospitality and nothing to delay a walker from passing through and entering the fell road beyond. This climbs steadily in surroundings that become quite austere, reaching more open country after a mile and a half between walls and fences. This is the end of the road for anything on wheels.

At this point, an isolated plantation will be noticed up on the hillside to the left, and if it can be reached without damaging walls it should be. Within the trees is the first highlight of the journey, Marble Steps Pot.

Marble Steps Pot – note the sheep

Not many potholes can be described as attractive, most being quite horrendous. Marble Steps, however, enclosed by a wall and under a canopy of foliage, looks almost inviting, the setting having a beauty in contrast to the desolate moorlands around. But amateur explorers should not be tempted to approach the hole too closely. Anybody falling in is likely to come out, if at all, as a corpse. It is 430 feet deep.

Incidentally, the wall coming down from Gragareth just beyond, marking the county boundary, has a stile that admits to Ireby Fell and The Cavern on the same contour. But this is not on today's agenda.

Returning to the end of the Masongill fell road, note Little Pot on the way down. Little is a relative term here, the floor of the hole being 85 feet below the surface.

The Turbary Road continues the fell road as a cart track free of constricting walls and maintaining a level contour with an uninterrupted view ahead. Progress is easy, without hazard or impediment, although minor potholes and shakeholes will be noticed in the rougher ground adjoining the track. Interest quickens after a mile when Turbary Pot appears by the side of the track. This gives a clue to the location of Swinsto Hole, five minutes north-west and to Simpson's Pot, over the wall in the next allotment east: their entrances are small and, masked by long grass, need a search but both admit to major cave systems.

Not needing any search, and impossible to miss, is a large crater bordering the track a little further on. This is Rowten Pot.

Rowten Pot

Rowten Pot compels a halt. This huge opening in the moor, as large as a tennis court, has been caused by a collapse of the surface coming to rest in a debris of fallen boulders twenty to thirty feet lower. This impressive scene is most safely surveyed from the north-eastern end where seats and couches are provided by the descending rocks; clearly in view here is the cave discharging water from Rowten Cave and Jingling Cave nearby. The south-western end of the hole is dangerous, a sinister shaft piercing the ground to a depth of 345 feet and open to receive bodies falling from the steep slopes around; from its dark base passages radiate like tentacles, one of them providing, after much crawling and diving through Satanic pools, a through route to an opening in the valley below.

Continuing along the track on a parallel course to Jingling Cave, which is unsuspected and unseen except at one point where it opens into daylight, Jingling Pot is reached, another gaping shaft described as superb in caving journals but not likely to be by timid observers. Other holes follow as the walk proceeds, the most notable being Bull Pot where the track passes above a low cliff.

Looking ahead from Bull Pot, a long plantation will be seen descending the hillside ahead. Leaving the track a pathless beeline may be made for the lower end of the trees, there ascending a short way to find Yordas Cave.

At last we have found a cave we may safely enter and explore.

57

The entrance to Yordas Cave

Yordas Cave is the legendary home of a legendary giant, Yordas, who had a liking for consuming little boys. These feastings have ceased, Yordas has gone, and little boys and people of all ages can now, in perfect safety, enter the roomy cavern where he lived. Some cautions must be mentioned, however: a good torch is essential, the floor is a carpet of clinging mud that sucks sandals and light shoes off the feet of visitors inadequately shod (wellingtons are the best footgear), and the ceiling is in places low enough to crack the skulls of unwary explorers.

The cave has long been known; one inscription bears the date 1653, and in Victorian times it was a showplace, a charge for admission being payable at Braida Garth farm down the valley. A neat stone arch and a flight of steps were built at the entrance and these have survived.

Inside, a slippery walk soon leads to a stream flowing across the line of approach: this, followed to the left, vanishes under a wall of rock, but a few paces upstream bring as a reward a vision of beauty. Here, through the portals of an inner chamber named the Chapter House, the stream is seen in the light of the torch entering the cave in a high and graceful waterfall. Visitors with imagination have given names to other limestone formations here: a pedestal of rock at the entrance to the inner chamber is variously known as The Pulpit and the Bishop's Throne, and the facing wall has a projection with a profile likened to the map of Wales. Curiosity satisfied, it is rather a relief to emerge from darkness to daylight.

Yordas Cave Waterfall

Visitors to Yordas Cave who have left their cars parked at or near Masongill must retrace their steps along the Turbary Road, a walk equally enjoyable when done in reverse. Travellers on foot, not so encumbered, have a choice of alternatives. They may go down the field below the cave to a gate on the Kingsdale road which, followed to the left, goes over a rise to Deepdale and Dent, and to the right leads down the valley to the more probable destination of Ingleton which has accommodation, shops, refreshments and bus services.

Kingsdale is quiet, almost silent, with two isolated farms sheltered by Gragareth in the west, and Whernside in the east. Only an occasional car disturbs the stillness, which is largely attributable to an absence of running water. True, there is a stream, Kingsdale Beck, draining the slopes of Whernside at the head of the valley and accompanying the road down but for much of its early journey it prefers to travel under rather than on its limestone bed and remains out of sight and hearing.

Keld Head

The road passes the farm of Braida Garth, across fields to the left, and a short mile further on Keld Head will be reached and passed unnoticed – unless a watch is kept for it over the roadside wall. Keld Head is a large, dark, deep and motionless pool of evil appearance: it is the uprising of all the streams falling into the Turbary Road pots which, after travelling underground, here return to daylight. It is joined here by Kingsdale Beck which now gets an infusion of energy and turns away to earn acclaim as a principal contributor to the charm of the walk around the Ingleton waterfalls.

The road continues south, climbing over a rise with a good retrospective view of the full length of Kingsdale and then makes a long descent to Thornton in Lonsdale after a branch turns off to the right for the A65 at Westhouse. At Thornton, a road to the left reaches Ingleton, a mile distant, passing on the way the entrance to the waterfalls and the obsolete railway viaduct.

5 THE GLENS AND WATERFALLS OF INGLETON

IF THERE IS IN THE north of England a more beautiful walk than the tour of the glens and waterfalls of Ingleton I have yet to discover it. In the space of four enchanting miles there is a rapid succession of lovely vistas of river scenery, of bewitching cascades and waterfalls in a woodland setting of great charm. For visitors from an urban background, here is a foretaste of paradise. . . . Two streams come down from a hilly hinterland and after a sedate infancy suddenly leap in a happy frolic through verdant surroundings to reach the village where they converge as the River Greta.

It is a little unfortunate that there are differences of opinion about the names of the two streams. In my young days, the western stream was known as the River Doe and the eastern the River Twiss: there was no apparent reason for the name Doe, but the name Twiss seemed to be derived from Twisleton Scar and Twisleton Hall below which it flowed. But by the time I had reached middle age, the Ordnance Survey had switched the names after an inconclusive local census, and for a few years the eastern stream appeared on their maps as the River Doe before being changed again – this time to the River Greta, having no doubt decided that the eastern stream was the principal of the two and really the source of the parent river. Confusion was compounded by local guidebooks and publications, the western stream being named therein as Kingsdale Beck with some justification, since it is a continuation of the stream of that name in its higher reaches; and the Twiss/Doe/Greta now appeared in print as Dale Beck.

But what's in a name? The Ingleton glens would be as sweet by any name, or none at all. They are a very popular attraction, a prime objective for countless visitors; they have put Ingleton on the map and brought a measure of prosperity to the village.

Signs TO THE WATERFALLS abound, all pointing to the usual entrance which is a short distance along the Thornton road from the centre of the village, passing over both streams on the way; they come together under the railway viaduct alongside. There is a large car park and admission to the walk is granted on payment of a small charge, whereupon visitors pass through a gateway into Arcadia. There is little need for directions: a much-trodden path goes upstream for two miles to Thornton Force, there crossing open ground to Beezley Farm for the return alongside the eastern stream. This emerges from the trees at a place where there was formerly a kiosk, from where an easy stroll leads past a swimming pool to the village.

MAP

Pecca Twin Falls

Holly Bush Spout

Thornton Force

Beezley Lower Falls

Beezley Upper Falls

Baxengill Gorge

Snow Falls

Cat Leap Falls

Ingleton Parish Church

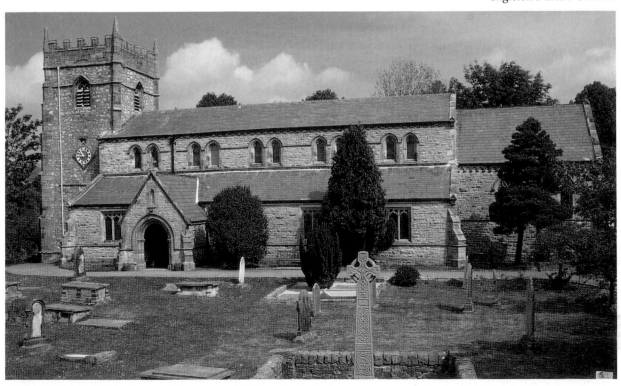

6 WHERNSIDE

WHERNSIDE RISES to 2419 feet above the sea and is the highest, largest and least attractive of the Three Peaks; indeed, unlike the other two, this great hill hardly deserves to be described as a peak, its smooth, bland outline nowhere suggesting a steep angular summit. Its huge bulk extends as an elevated ridge declining to valley level at Dentdale in the north and Ingleton in the south, a distance of eight miles: it is an upthrust of barren ground with pretensions to attractiveness only at the extremities. It is bounded by Kingsdale and Deepdale in the west and the Ingleton—Hawes road in the east, and may be ascended, with little impediment and not much pleasure, from any direction. The reward for doing so has been stated as revealing a view of the towers of York Minster, a claim difficult to believe without visual evidence. The highest point has an Ordnance column in the shelter of a sturdy wall but, apart from the view, which includes a bird's-eye sighting of the Ribblehead railway viaduct far below, there is little inducement to linger.

Two features, however, give Whernside a measure of distinction: on the northern approach three large tarns are passed, a surprise in a district notable for its absence of standing water, and on the southern slopes around and below the 1200-ft contour is a belt of limestone with an attendant necklace of potholes. Whernside feeds the two streams that entrance visitors to Ingleton with their succession of lovely waterfalls. In bad weather conditions, it has a lifeline to safety, a long and unbroken wall crossing the summit and continuing as a reliable guide to the environs of Ingleton. As an exercise for the legs, Whernside excels but in immediate interest cannot compare with the neighbouring Ingleborough and Penyghent. Its summit, however, is the highest point on the popular Three Peaks marathon walk and receives many visitors in varying stages of exhaustion; others, with no such aspirations, will derive little enjoyment from the ascent unless the day is calm and clear.

Opposite *Whernside from White Scar Clints*
Right *The summit of Whernside, looking to Ingleborough*

65

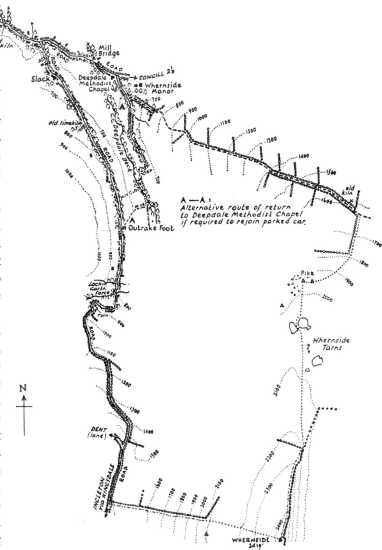

Ascent from Dentdale

The ascent of Whernside from the north has two advantages over other routes: first, for much of the journey the lovely valley of Dentdale remains in sight to counter the increasing harshness of the terrain and, secondly, an alternative route of return is available.

From Dent, the street opposite the Sedgwick memorial is taken; this soon becomes a country lane followed for a mile and a half to Deepdale Methodist Chapel, ignoring a signposted branch to Ingleton after a mile. At the chapel, there is space to park a car.

Up the side road at the chapel an old track, walled at first, branches to the left, passes behind the grounds of Whernside Manor and climbs gradually across the lower slopes of Whernside: this is an ancient right of way probably more in use in packhorse days than now. At its highest point, a turn to the right up a pathless incline leads to the subsidiary height of Pike which has two cairns; from here the route, still pathless, heads due south, passing the three Whernside Tarns and rises to join a wall coming up from the left, this being kept alongside to the summit.

The alternative route of return descends the rough western slope aiming for the top of the Kingsdale—Deepdale road, which soon comes into view, and there turns right. Here an old lane branching left offers an exhilarating return to Dent, free of traffic. Or Dent may be reached by continuing down the road into Deepdale. If a car has been left at the chapel, a more direct way to it may be made by turning down into the valley from Outrake Foot.

Prospect of Dentdale from Pike

Below *Whernside Tarn and the summit*

Ascent from Ribblehead

The Three Peaks route may be followed to the summit from Ribblehead. A cart track leaves the Ingleton—Hawes road east of the inn and passes below the railway viaduct to Winterscales, whence a steep beeline is made to the top. This route is direct but becomes tedious in the later stages.

A longer but more interesting approach is possible by leaving the cart track at the viaduct and keeping along the east side of the railway; join the track from Winterscales to Dentdale by passing over a bridge near the entrance to Blea Moor tunnel. Across the railway, Force Gill comes into view and is followed upstream, departing from the track. Force Gill has two fine waterfalls which would earn an admiring patronage if they were better known. The stream curves left into the Greensett area; here there is a cave and three small potholes and, surprisingly, a large tarn. A short climb from the tarn leads to the ridge wall, the summit then being within easy reach on the left.

Blea Moor tunnel, Ribblehead

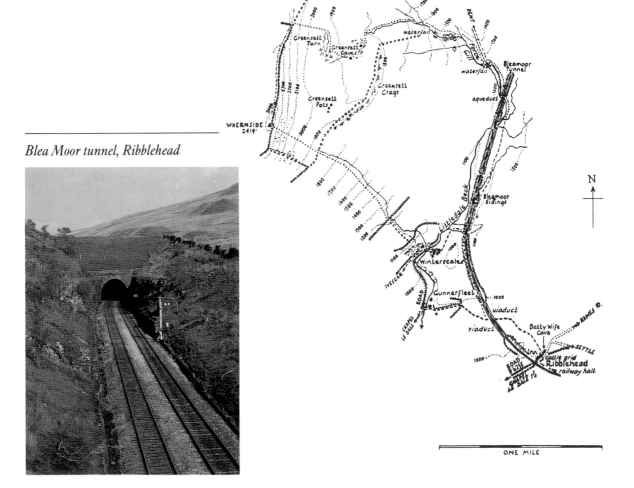

Lower Falls of Force Gill

Above *Upper Falls of Force Gill*

Below *Greensett Tarn*

Ascent from Ingleton

The walk to Whernside's top from Ingleton is a full day's expedition, a test of stamina, with little of immediate interest in the later stages. A disadvantage is the absence of any convenient alternative route of return, steps having to be retraced exactly unless a kind friend can be persuaded to take his car to the Hill Inn at Chapel-le-Dale and wait there. There is no enjoyment in climbing Whernside in mist or rain but if overtaken by bad weather, a perfect lifeline to safety is provided by a five-mile ridge wall that leads infallibly back to the environs of Ingleton.

From the village centre, the Thornton road descends sharply initially and when it levels, a side road called Oddies Lane turns off to the right. This passes a medley of buildings before commencing a steady climb, fringed by trees, to Twisleton Hall, a farm. On the way, the ruins of an old nunnery can be seen on the left. Cars may be taken as far as the Hall and, with permission, parked there, a concession especially appreciated when returning. Beyond the farm buildings, the waterfalls path is joined and briefly followed to the left until a path forks to the right to come alongside a wall that will be a constant companion for the rest of the journey and in misty conditions must be kept in sight. The path, climbing thus far, veers away a little and keeps to a parallel course along the broad top of Scales Moor where there are scattered manifestations of limestone, notably a fluted pothole near the path. Over the wall, overlooking Kingsdale, is a tight concentration of potholes, some of great depth, but if Whernside's summit is to be reached in good time they must be considered out of bounds. Above the 1300-ft contour, the zone of limestone ends, and with it

Ruins of the Nunnery, Ingleton

much of the interest in the walk. Ahead, the wall goes on interminably for mile after mile to the distant swelling on the horizon marking the summit. One cannot help but feel apprehensive that every step forward will have to be reversed on the return journey when energy is flagging. At long length, the slope of the ridge, so far imperceptible, becomes more pronounced, raising hopes that the summit is near – but disappointment follows when, on topping the rise, it is seen to be succeeded by others. There is still a long mile to go to the ultimate top, and even the wall, so far dead straight, falters into a zigzag to relieve its boredom. But all things come to an end and the Ordnance column on the highest point at last comes into sight and is thankfully reached.

After a study of the extensive panorama, if a return is to be made direct to Ingleton, the route of ascent must be reversed exactly.

The Standing Stone on Scales Moor

The Fluted Pothole

WHERNSIDE 2419'

High Pike

Low Pike

Sand Beds Head Pike

Combe Scar

Broadrake

Bruntscar

Hodge Hole

cattle grids

Ellerbeck

cattle grid

West Fell

ford

farm

CHAPEL LE DALE

Philpin

ROAD B6255   HAWES 11¼

cattle grids

(INGLETON)   Hill Inn

Rigg Side

old sheepfold

Scales Moor

N

Standing Stone

fluted pothole

Ewes Top

shelter

KINGSDALE

Twisleton Scar

WATERFALLS WALK

Scar End   Twisleton Hall

nunnery (ruin)

farm road

CHAPEL LE DALE 3

Oddies Lane (motor road)

ONE MILE

Meal Bank

WATERFALLS WALK

former railways

old quarry

River Greta

Ingleton

HAWES 16

Bus Station

Looking south to Ribblehead from Whernside

If advance arrangements have been made for a car to be waiting at the Hill Inn in Chapel-le-Dale to give a return to Ingleton in effortless comfort, the route followed by Three Peaks walkers from Whernside's summit is the best to adopt. This descends alongside the ridge wall over High Pike and Low Pike and then diverges due south in a direct line down a steep slope to Bruntscar. Tired legs, sore feet and shortage of time should not deter an inspection of the unusual sight at the rear of the now unoccupied farmhouse here: in the backyard, only a short way from the buildings, is the impressive entrance to Bruntscar Cave which penetrates half a mile under the hillside. From here, farm roads and lanes give an easy passage down to the main road and the Hill Inn. If the car is there and unattended, the driver will probably be inside.

The area around Chapel-le-Dale is scenically attractive and prolific in surprises: it is a wonderland deserving a separate expedition and a leisurely exploration.

A line of farmhouses shelters below the steep eastern slopes of Whernside, distant from the main road and rarely disturbed by tourists and sightseers. Linked by lanes and quiet roads, there is a pleasant circular walk free of traffic (cars are not welcome) and without danger from bulls, dogs and irate farmers. Starting and finishing at the Hill Inn, the walk passes through a district liberally pockmarked with caves and potholes of which Bruntscar and Gatekirk Cave are especially worth a halt to inspect the outsides.

The graveyard of the modest little church at Chapelle-Dale is the last resting place of the many men who died from illness and disease during the construction of the Ribblehead railway viaduct in the 1870s as a result of the privations they suffered. They are commemorated by a tablet in the wall inside the church.

Behind the church, which is set back from the main road and screened by trees, a sequestered lane soon passes the large hole of Hurtle Pot. Further along is Jingle Pot, another large crater of no great depth. A short distance beyond is the best-known cave in this area: Weathercote Cave is a huge rift, once a showplace with a charge for admission. It has a flight of steps leading down into the depths, and its main feature is a high waterfall that emerges from behind a wedged boulder known as Mohammed's Coffin. From the depths, the scene is very impressive. Since the times of Victorian patronage, explorations have opened up half a mile of underground passages leading from the floor of the cave, but these later discoveries are for experts only: amateurs should venture no further than the bottom of the steps.

Above *Bruntscar Cave*

Below *St. Leonard's Church*

73

Left *Hurtle Pot*
Bottom left *Jingle Pot*
Below *Weathercote Cave: note Mohammed's Coffin just abo*
waterfall

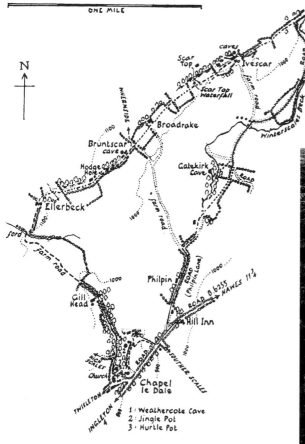

A line of farmhouse shelters below the steep eastern slopes of Whernside, distant from the main road and rarely disturbed by tourists and sightseers. Linked by lanes and quiet roads, there is a pleasant circular walk free of traffic (cars are not welcome) and without danger from bulls, dogs and irate farmers. Starting and finishing at the Hill Inn, the walk passes through a district liberally pockmarked with caves and potholes of which Bruntscar and Gatekirk Cave are especially worth a halt to inspect the outsides. Near Gatekirk Cave is the resurfance of the underground streams draining from Whernside; here they emerge into daylight.

Above right *Gatekirk Cave*
Right *The resurgence at Gatekirk*

7 INGLEBOROUGH

INGLEBOROUGH HAS BEEN a favourite mountain of mine ever since I first climbed it as a young man. Over many years I have ascended the steep final slopes to the broad top often. I have climbed it from all sides, every time making new discoveries, finding new surprises and delights and, let me confess, secret places from which I have recoiled in horror. Ingleborough is a wonderful mountain for the amateur explorer, its surface being perforated by hundreds of holes, some gaping chasms, some mere slits in the ground not easy to locate, and for underground enthusiasts it offers a lifetime of excitement and adventure. Shame on the Ordnance Survey for giving it the name of Ingleborough Hill on some of their maps: it is every inch a mountain and, although not the highest in England as was once thought and is overtopped by many others, one of the grandest.

The top thousand feet of height is a superstructure composed mainly of millstone grit and shales, with a summit fringe of low cliffs decorated in places by purple saxifrage. It rests on a massive plinth of carboniferous limestone around the 1300-ft contour, this being based at valley level on impervious rock. The summit of Ingleborough is a place of legend and history. There are still traces of hut circles attributed to an Iron Age occupation and, at the time of the Roman invasion, the local patriots, the Brigantes, established a hill fort to resist the foreign legions; an ancient rampart wall, built around the perimeter of the summit and almost half a mile in circumference, has survived the centuries although it is now crumbled and has many gaps. Nearer our own time, in 1830, when the extensive manor of Ingleton changed hands, the new owner had a tower intended as a hospice erected on the summit, made from stone pillaged from the wall and the foundations of the huts. The edifice was short lived: on the day of the opening ceremony, the assembled crowd of visitors got out of control during the festivities and dismantled the building, reducing it to the great heap of stones to be seen today. Nearby, a wall shelter intended as a wind break, was fitted with a view indicator in 1953 to commemorate the coronation of Elizabeth II.

The summit is 2373 feet above the sea, not a great altitude, but to the many pilgrims who climb to it time and time again, it is a stepping stone to heaven.

Opposite Ingleborough from the limestone pavement of White Scars   *Below* The ruins on Ingleborough summit

The wind break on the summit

For me and the growing number of cavers and potholers, the fascination of Ingleborough is centred on the band of limestone at and below mid-height. Here, on all sides where this softer rock breaks or underlies the surface, streams flowing down from the upper slopes, aided and abetted by heavy rain, have, ever since the landscape was formed, been slowly penetrating the ground and eroding a honeycomb of underground caverns and passages of amazing dimensions. Some extend in total darkness for miles and reveal displays of delicate carvings and formations that make water-action the greatest of all natural sculptors.

These apertures in the surface vary in size and character: no two are alike, some are open and vertical gulfs, others mere fissures in the surface rocks not easy to locate; many have cave entrances that invite a limited exploration. These openings can be found by ramblers who prefer daylight to darkness and, like me, like to wander in search of them, but the black labyrinth to which they lead, the complex network below ground, is reserved exclusively for those experienced in subterranean travel, hardy adventurers who risk rockfalls and flooding to satisfy an insatiable curiosity to go where few men have been before, to see what few men have seen before. The major cave systems invariably end hundreds of feet below the surface in deep, silent and unmoving pools known as sumps, these being the ultimate objectives of exploration. There is no way forward beyond; the sumps represent finality. Many of the larger systems have been mapped meticulously and show an intricate pattern of passages, often crossing at different levels and branching in all directions in weird disarray.

Caving, of course, does nothing for pristine clothing, but the bedraggled and apparent roughnecks seen in the streets of Ingleton after a hard day can afford to ignore the caustic comments of observers: they know a wonderful world their critics will never see. I take my hat off to them.

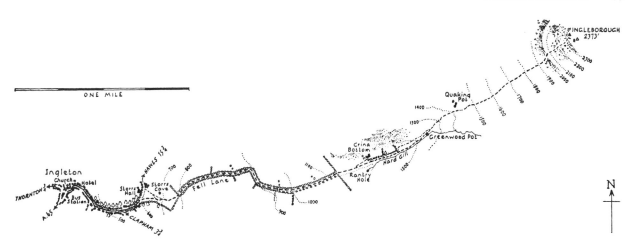

Ascent from Ingleton

The most popular route of ascent is from Ingleton and this is the one invariably followed by first-time visitors although it is not the best, and the much-trodden path is well populated on most days of the year. Those who pass along it without divergence, however, remain unaware of the interesting features that give Ingleborough its unique distinction, hazards and difficulties also being avoided on the straightforward climb.

The B6255 road from Ingleton to Hawes is followed to a large open area of ground, Storrs Common, where it is possible to leave cars. Here a track turns off to the right to mount the gentle slope where, at mid-height, a short detour to the left reveals Storrs Cave. Two entrances, an upper and a lower, descend easily to join under a natural bridge where a passage descends into darkness but becomes choked by boulders.

The track continues uphill, soon levelling to pass between the walls of Fell Lane, going forward but constricted for a long and uninteresting mile with Ingleborough out of sight and little worthy of note along the way apart from a large rock embedded in the lane and known as Giant's Grave.

The lower entrance of Storrs Cave

Giant's Grave

A final steep rise in the lane is littered by stones fallen from the walls; these end suddenly to reveal a fine view of Ingleborough directly ahead, its massive dome seen across a wide depression occupied by the lonely dwelling of Crina Bottom in a walled enclosure among sheltering trees. At this point tedium vanishes, a pleasant path succeeds the walls and descends easily to the depression, the objective growing in stature with every step forward.

The path passes alongside the boundary wall of Crina to enter a disturbed terrain of minor undulations in the vicinity of Hard Gill, the potholes here draining into the extremities of White Scar Cave far underground.

Ingleborough, from Crina Bottom

Quaking Pot

Further on, as the path steepens, a hollow on the moor to the left may be noted. This is Quaking Pot, a sinkhole with a stream descending into the depths where passages extend southwards for a third of a mile to a depth measured as 467 feet. This, when I first saw it, seemed to be no more than a pleasant crater, but later explorations by experts have classed it as one of the most severe in the district. The path, here still a thousand feet below the top, becomes very rough as the gradient increases, the final scramble through a breach in the summit cliffs over the debris of erosion being sufficiently arduous to justify a prolonged rest when the flat top is at last reached.

The summit cliffs of Ingleborough

The Ingleton—Chapel-le-Dale road

The highway between Ingleton and Chapel-le-Dale, a distance of four miles, overlays a Roman road subsequently adopted as part of the Lancaster—Richmond turnpike and now simply classed as the B6255. It traverses a glacial valley enclosed by Whernside and Ingleborough; its attractiveness is rather marred by the debris of disused quarries but it does have features of special interest along the way.

The road out of Ingleton spirals to gain height and after a mile straightens course and passes Skirwith Farm. Across the road at this point, at the head of a stream, is Skirwith Cave. It penetrates Ingleborough for half a mile; formerly open to the public, it is now closed.

A mile further on is White Scar Cave, the best known, most advertised and heavily patronised in the district and a compulsive halt for coaches and cars; indeed, the large parking space, the roadside signs and shopping facilities make it a commercial rather than a show cave. Guided parties are taken into the cave on payment of an admission charge, the interior being illuminated by electricity that reveals waterfalls and many named formations. The section open to the public, negotiated in comfort, is only a fraction of the total extent of the cave which worms its way forward, receiving thirty streams in a tortuous journey of four miles. This underground showplace was unsuspected until 1923 when a Cambridge undergraduate named Long noticed a small aperture in the hillside and, upon investigation by crawling into it, soon found himself entering a more commodious passage which in turn led to a magnificent cavern drained by a dancing stream and liberally decorated with delicate stalactites and natural carvings. His discovery aroused great local interest, explorations followed and an artificial entrance, the one now used by the public, was tunnelled into the limestone to give easier access; this connected with the original route beyond its initial difficulties. Despite the crowds and an exterior complex of manager's house, souvenir shop, ticket office and litter baskets, White Scar Cave is an enthralling experience. Inflation here has been rampant, the charge for admission having increased sixty-fold since I was a lad.

The complex at White Scar Cave

God's Bridge, Chapel-le-Dale

After a further mile towards Chapel-le-Dale, a track turns off the road to the left and goes down to the beck in the valley bottom, arriving at a section roofed by a natural arch of considerable length. The stream bed below is normally dry as the water percolates through at a lower level. This is another God's Bridge and the stream it shelters is known both as Dale Beck and Chapel Beck.

After another mile, Chapel-le-Dale is reached, an oasis of greenery in a bleak landscape. Here Ingleborough, thus far hidden by high limestone scars bordering the road, comes into view, looking aggressively steep and even hostile. Chapel-le-Dale has many natural attractions but these must be forsworn if the day's objective for those walking is Ingleborough's summit; the rising road should be followed further to the Hill Inn, a renowned hostelry dispensing manna from heaven to weary Three Peaks walkers.

The Hill Inn, Chapel-le-Dale

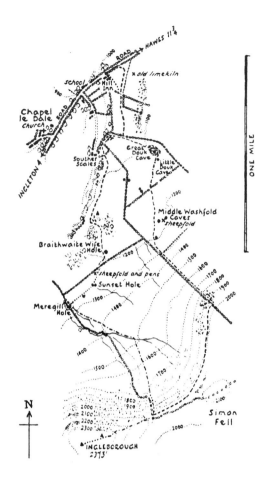

Ascent from Chapel-le-Dale

A short distance up the road from the Hill Inn, a bridleway turns off to the right and, with Ingleborough looming directly in front, passes along an easy terrace to reach a gate in a cross-wall after half a mile. Immediately beyond, a track goes left to a large depression enclosed by a wall and furnished with trees and shrubs. A simple path descends into the crater at the western end to reveal the place of debouchure of Great Douk Cave, a stream emerging in a small waterfall: a picture for the camera. The interior of the cave soon admits daylight from a vertical shaft on the moor above, Little Douk Pot, and then meanders in darkness for half a mile to its entrance at Middle Washfold, due south over the wall in the next allotment where an isolated outcrop of limestone makes a white scar on the dark moor. I have always found Middle Washfold to be a place of fascinating interest. Here there is a sheepfold with a stream disappearing into a fissure alongside its northern end. A few yards west is the dry entrance to the caves, which novices like myself can safely probe until confronted by difficulties; daylight is admitted from manholes in the surface clints. Nearby, in the south, is a sink that also connects, as do the other openings, with the Great Douk Cave system. I am always loth to leave Middle Washfold: unlike many cave surrounds, it is friendly, a pleasant study in green and white. I like it.

Above *Great Douk Cave*

Below *Middle Washfold Cave – the wet entrance* and, right, *the dry entrance*

The wall running up to the skyline beyond Middle Washfold points the way to the summit of Ingleborough and is the route usually followed by Three Peaks walkers, but others not committed to this arduous marathon, especially if inspired by what they have seen at Great Douk and Middle Washfold, may wish to linger on the easy ground below the steepening slopes. If so, their next place of call should be Sunset Hole, found south-west towards the end of the next allotment. There are two entrances, one admitting a stream and the other dry; they soon join, a roomy passage then continuing into the darkness. This is a cave very accommodating for beginners in speleology and indeed for ordinary walkers with no such aspirations who, aided only by a torch, can penetrate quite easily for a hundred yards without meeting any difficulty. When the accompanying stream drops over a ledge, it is a signal to retreat and return to daylight. Enthusiasm should not be allowed to overrule common sense: beyond the point of return, the cave continues for a further half-mile, dropping in pitches to a depth of 250 feet. By following the course of the stream overland and looking over an intervening wall, the immense crater of Braithwaite Wife Hole will next be seen.

Meregill Hole and Ingleborough

The biggest attraction hereabouts for seasoned cavers is, however, located over the wall south-west of Sunset Hole, where an awesome rift in the hillside admits a stream. This is Meregill Hole which has been descended to a depth of 565 feet, giving it the distinction of being the deepest of all. A feature is an underground lake known as the Mere.

Ingleborough is seen from Meregill Hole at close range and its appearance is daunting, steepening slopes topped by cliffs being a deterrent to intentions to reach the summit. Walkers who have visited the caves and potholes already mentioned, and enjoyed doing so, will be sorely tempted to stay on the limestone shelf and search for the dozen or more other similar openings hereabouts and then return to the Hill Inn for refreshment. Others of iron resolution, having announced at breakfast their determination to climb Ingleborough that day, will have to save face by continuing the ascent. This they can most easily accomplish by following the wall between Sunset and Meregill upwards to the skyline depression to the left of the summit, a dull climb with no views other than those in retrospect until the ridge is reached and a turn to the right made to the top. On the final stage, the Ribblehead viaduct comes into view in a widening landscape and Whernside is seen in full stature, assuming a majesty not usually attributed to it from other directions.

Whernside, from Ingleborough

Ascent from Newby

The ascent to Ingleborough's top from Newby, although direct, is the least attractive route, being pathless most of the way and unfriendly underfoot on the rough and featureless crossing of Ingleborough Common. But at mid-height, on Newby Moss, there is a purple patch of excitement in a tight concentration of potholes, some of great depth, others ornamented around their surface openings by shrubs and heather, and pretty enough to make one wish they could be transported to the back garden at home. Newby Moss merits a leisurely exploration but the broad ridge beyond cannot be recommended to walkers who travel for pleasure.

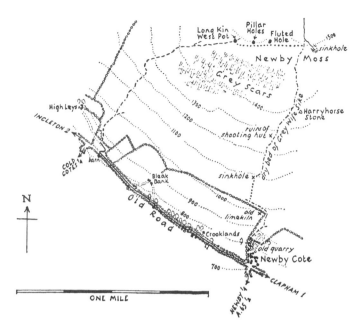

Newby is a quiet village between the busy A65 and the old road linking Ingleton and Clapham with road access to both. At Newby Cote, a detached farming community on the old road, a track leads up the hillside and when it ends, its direction can be maintained by continuing upwards alongside the stream bed of Grey Wife Sike, which is normally dry. It is a dull plod, although interest is momentarily revived by a recognition of Harryhorse Stone nearby. But around the 1400-ft contour, there is excitement in plenty although it is not at first apparent. The limestone scars seen on the left during the ascent here give place to a moorland shelf inclined at an easier gradient which, on investigation, is found to be perforated by a line of potholes. Slightly to the east of the Sike is a long shakehole opening into Newby Moss Pot, 315 feet in depth and therefore to be avoided; and there are other mantraps nearby. But it is to the west of the Sike on the same contour that most interest is centred. If navigation is correct, Fluted Hole, Pillar Holes and Long Kin West Pot are on the same line of approach with smaller holes intruding nearby. The dangers of too close inspection are obvious, and Long Kin West especially calls for caution: this hole descends vertically for over 500 feet from a rock bridge across its top carrying a track from Cold Cotes on the old road. If life is considered precious keep well away. If the contour is followed around a curve to the north overlooking Crina Bottom, a dozen more holes will be found. There is enough interest on Newby Moss to evaporate all thoughts of continuing upwards to climb Ingleborough.

Harryhorse Stone

Walkers who have no desire to locate the potholes of Newby Moss and refuse to be deflected from their intention to reach the top of Ingleborough can best achieve their objective by continuing upwards, guided by Grey Wife Sike across the rough and rising terrain of Ingleborough Common. Aim for the knoll of Little Ingleborough where a path coming up from Gaping Gill will be joined for the last easy half-mile to the summit.

Right *Fluted Hole*
Below left *Long Kin West Pot*
Below right *Pillar Holes*

A corner of Clapham

Ascent from Clapham

Ingleborough is not in view from Clapham and the near presence of the mountain, so dominant when seen from other directions, is not suspected by the many admiring and envious visitors who parade the charming byways of this most delightful of Yorkshire villages. Nevertheless, here is the key, a golden one, to the route to the summit that excels all others in sustained beauty and interest.

Clapham is an ancient settlement with roots in Saxon times and the mellowed stones of its buildings blend in perfect harmony with a background of limestone scars and lovely woodlands. Happily the village is now bypassed and so spared the torture of heavy traffic, a blessing appreciated by the grateful residents. Two quiet roads lead up to the head of the village; between them, still bubbling with excitement after a remarkable journey from the depths of Gaping Gill, is Clapham Beck, fringed by trees and crossed by five bridges, on its way to join the River Wenning. Alongside the parish church of St James and embowered in trees, the beck discharges in a large waterfall from an artificial lake above in the grounds of Ingleborough Hall, long the home of the Farrer family and now a special school. The most renowned of the family was Reginald who won international fame as a collector of rare and exotic plants from the countries of the Far East and whose name lives on in several of his discoveries. The Farrers were generous benefactors, providing the inhabitants with electricity from a private turbine at the waterfall and contributing generously to the common good, but most notably in the lovely environs they created by planting natural woodlands, and constructing a lake and other amenities on their extensive estate nearby. The Farrers served Clapham well.

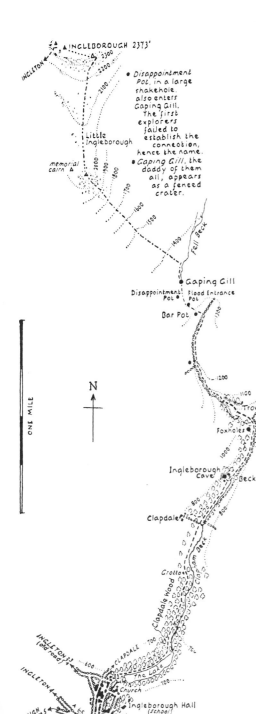

Ingleborough from Clapham is more than a simple walk. It is better described as a full day's expedition, and those who undertake it need to be well-provisioned and should allow ample time to see the many natural attractions along the way.

At a cottage at the top end of the village, permission is granted, on payment of a small charge, to enter the grounds of Ingleborough Hall. A curving drive amongst trees leads up to the side of the lake and continues thence along the edge of the water in beautiful surroundings richly endowed with lovely trees planted by the Farrers in the days long ago when woodlands were intended for ornamental display and were allowed to develop to full maturity with no thought of slaughtering them for profit. Here the magnificent oaks and beeches are twice graced by their reflections in the still waters of the lake.

The lake

The grotto

Past the end of the lake a limestone grotto is reached, affording shelter but not now maintained in pristine condition. Beyond, where the private grounds are left, a track from Clapdale Farm is joined and the walk continues in a more open environment along the valley of Clapham Beck to the massive limestone cliff where Ingleborough Cave, sometimes called Clapham Cave, opens to daylight. This is a show cave, open to the public when a guide is in attendance; the charge for admittance is rewarded by a splendid display of natural carvings and formations and many named features.

Beyond the public sector, the cave becomes increasingly difficult, and is accessible only to experts. By meticulous surveying and mapping over many years, exploration of the cave beyond its earliest known extremities – to connect with underground passages coming down from Gaping Gill a mile away – had been charted to within a short distance. This uncharted section was finally penetrated after arduous effort in 1983 and the mystery of the missing link solved. There is now a through route underground between Gaping Gill and Ingleborough Cave but only for brave men.

The entrance to Ingleborough Cave

Above *The resurgence at Beck Head*
Below *Trow Gill*

A few yards beyond the entrance to Ingleborough Cave, a strong resurgence emerges from the base of a cliff on the left. This is the stream that falls into Gaping Gill on the moor above as Fell Beck and, after a tortuous journey through the bowels of the earth, returns to daylight here with the name of Clapham Beck. A picturesque bridge carries the path across the water to continue very pleasantly to the head of the valley, and here it turns a corner into Trow Gill. In the outcrops on the left at this point is the Foxholes, a cave that has produced evidences of Neolithic occupation.

Trow Gill is dry, a grass slope rising and narrowing to a breach in the cliffs at the top, a passage through it being made up a tumble of boulders. There seems little doubt that Trow Gill once brought down a stream, this entering as a waterfall at the gap now occupied by boulders, and this theory is confirmed by the dry channel coming directly down to it from the heights above.

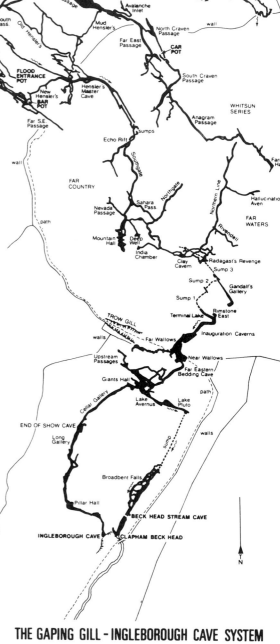

Above Trow Gill, the path rises gradually alongside a wall and after half a mile reaches a stile admitting to the open moorland on the left. Over the wall, a much-trodden path makes immediate acquaintance with Bar Pot, a large opening; from here passages and shafts descend to join the Gaping Gill system deep underground. Further along the path, also on the right, are small fissures in the clints that may be passed unnoticed: one of these, Flood Entrance Pot, was the first alternative way down into Gaping Gill when the main shaft was impassable. Then the path turns due north to the daddy of all potholes, Gaping Gill.

Gaping Gill should be approached with caution, and children and dogs kept on a tight rein. A large vertical shaft plunges suddenly and without prior warning at the bottom of a steep-sided and unfenced crater; a slip could not be checked and a falling body would be swallowed by the black gulf and not come to rest until hitting the boulder floor 340 feet below. The approach to the hole should always be made along the stream bed and halted a safe distance from the brink.

Descents by the caving clubs are usually made from a winch at the main shaft after the stream has been diverted by a barrier into a side passage, the Rat Hole, on the west bank. The shaft widens as it descends to form an immense cavern said to be large enough to contain a cathedral. From its floor, passages radiate for seven miles in all directions – as shown on the plan of the underground system facing. On this plan, the missing link with Ingleborough Cave, since found, is indicated by a broken line.

A newly-blazed path leaves the Gaping Gill area and climbs to the ridge high above in the west, there passing over Little Ingleborough to reach the main summit half a mile further on. The final stage goes up a smooth incline that appears to have been man-made, possibly to ease the passage of materials for the erections on the top.

THE GAPING GILL - INGLEBOROUGH CAVE SYSTEM

Plan based on B.P.C./B.S.A./E.C.C./H.W.C.P.C./L.U.C.C./L.U.S.S./N.P.C./U.L.S.A./Y.R.C. sur

From Northern Caves (Volume 3)
© *Dalesman Publishing Co. Ltd.*

Above *Ingleborough, from Little Ingleborough*

Below *Gaping Gill*

The tunnels

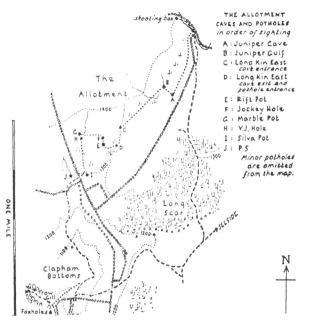

THE ALLOTMENT
CAVES AND POTHOLES
in order of sighting

A : Juniper Cave
B : Juniper Gulf
C : Long Kin East
      cave entrance
D : Long Kin East
      cave exit and
      pothole entrance
E : Rift Pot
F : Jockey Hole
G : Marble Pot
H : V.J. Hole
I : Silva Pot
J : P.5

*Minor potholes
are omitted
from the map.*

THE ALLOTMENT

A tour of great interest to walkers who like to search for holes in the ground, but having no appeal to others who do not, is provided by a visit to the Allotment, an area of moorland adjacent to the Gaping Gill complex. This may be reached from Horton in Ribblesdale, but more pleasantly from Clapham by taking the bridleway east of the church. This unexpectedly burrows beneath the grounds of Ingleborough Hall in two long tunnels. Beyond, a lane – called Long Lane – branches left and comes to an end after two miles with Clapham Beck down on the left and the limestone scars of Norber up on the right. From the end of the lane, a circular walk may be made as suggested on the map, starting along the path to Selside but turning off after a mile to aim due north for the far end of the Allotment wall.

In the Allotment, by keeping the wall at close range, a line of potholes will be seen, the most significant of these being Juniper Gulf which descends for over 400 feet. Others follow, the most interesting for a novice explorer being Long Kin East Cave which can be entered safely by either of two entrances, a wet and a dry, and with the help of a torch it can be penetrated by easy walking along a roomy stream passage for 200 yards. But no further. The cave continues but then suddenly falls to horrendous depths and a retreat must be made to the point of entry.

Nearby are Rift Pot and Jockey Hole, fit subjects for nightmares. Through a gate in the wall at the end of the Allotment, deep potholes forming part of the Gaping Gill complex come immediately into view. A direct return to the end of Long Lane may be made by crossing the depression of Clapham Bottoms.

An alternative and more interesting route of return to Clapham is available by following the wall west, turning south, from the end of the Allotment, passing other satellites of Gaping Gill, descending Trow Gill and joining the pleasant path along the valley of Clapham Beck.

Above *Juniper Gulf*
Below *The entrance to Long Kin East Cave*

Top *Rift Pot*
Middle *Jockey Hole*
Bottom *Long Kin East Pot*

Ascent from Horton in Ribblesdale

Walkers on the Three Peaks marathon usually start from Horton in Ribblesdale and do the journey anti-clockwise, visiting Penyghent, Whernside and Ingleborough in that order and returning to Horton from the last named by a route that approximates to a beeline.

This beeline may be reversed and used as a route of ascent from Horton but until a clear path has been formed by foot-traffic over the rough higher ground, it is not a way to be preferred to other more pleasant routes of ascent: apart from an exciting interlude midway, the climb becomes tedious.

A path leaves Horton railway station, a large quarry giving an industrial background to the first stage of the climb which continues to rise along the geological fault of Sulber Nick to come alongside the Allotment wall at around the 1300-ft contour. Here interest is revived by the sight of Sulber Pot and intensified a few yards further where, in a hollow, Nick Pot is seen; alternative entrances combine below the surface at the top of a vertical shaft that falls sheer to a depth of 370 feet. The wall alongside is then followed up around the curve of Simon Fell and the top of Ingleborough is reached from the north-east.

THE ALUM POT CAVE SYSTEM

Alum Pot and its attendant caves were amongst the earliest to attract the curiosity of local explorers and they have been known in intimate detail since the middle of last century. Alum Pot itself could not fail to be noticed by the first settlers in the district, its yawning gulf constituting an obvious danger to both man and beast; in the course of time, a wall was built around it and trees planted to indicate its position. The hole is of huge dimensions and descends to a depth of 340 feet. It is fed

Above *Sulber Pot*
Below *Nick Pot*

by a stream that enters at its south end and by waterfalls emerging from caves in its northern wall. Alum Pot is comprehended at a single fearful glance, and it is the intricacies of its cave system that are of most interest to sight-seeing visitors.

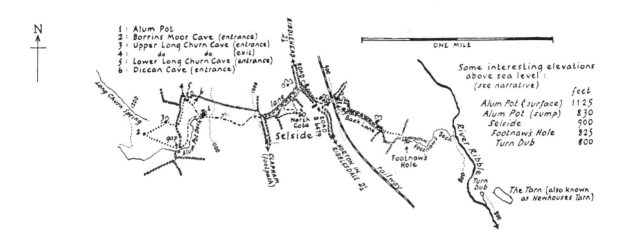

The hamlet of Selside, on the road linking Ribblehead and Horton in Ribblesdale, is the nearest and most convenient starting point for the short walk to Alum Pot, half a mile away. A lane branches south-west from the top end of the buildings and at a right-angled corner turns away as a footpath to Clapham. Alum Pot is straight ahead in a plantation of trees and is reached on foot in a few minutes, arriving there simultaneously with Alum Pot Beck which enters the plantation and disappears into the depths.

Alum Pot is palpably not a place for novices to explore, and for the uninitiated most interest will be found in the north corner of the same field.

Selside

The entrance to Upper Long Churn Cave

On the higher slopes of Park Fell overlooking Alum Pot, water bubbles from the peat and takes shape as a stream known as Long Churn Spring, coursing down the hillside through a morass to reach a limestone scar on the 1200-ft contour, where it disappears into Upper Long Churn Cave. This may be entered but progress is soon halted by a waterslide into a deep pool. In the darkness, the stream trends north-east and if this direction is followed through the outcropping limestone overland, the exit of the cave is reached at the top of the walled enclosure above Alum Pot. No water emerges from the exit, the stream electing to sink in its bed a short distance inside.

A few yards from the exit of Upper Long Churn Cave and at a lower level is the entrance to Lower Long Churn Cave; this may also be safely explored, the gloom being diffused by daylight entering a fissure in the roof, to the point where the stream sinking in Upper Long Churn Cave enters in a waterfall after a short journey underground. The stream proves precocious, soon again switching allegiance by departing to the next cave down the field, Diccan Cave: bereft of its water, Lower Long Churn continues with increasing difficulties and enters Alum Pot on its north side.

Diccan Cave is a much tougher proposition. The entrance is dry but soon becomes low, developing into a crawl where the stream from Lower Long Churn is admitted. Then follows a series of vertical pitches

Above *The entrance to Lower Long Churn Cave, looking to Alum Pot*

descending 355 feet in total in the company of the stream, which finally plunges in a high waterfall to the lower recesses of Alum Pot. This cave, also known as Diccan Pot, must be regarded as absolutely out of bounds for all but hardy and experienced cavers.

The vagaries of the stream are not ended when it finally debouches into the silent pool at the bottom of Alum Pot. Chemical tests have proved that the water from this sump makes a further journey underground, passing beneath the road and railway at Selside, then under the River Ribble, to reappear in a large pool, Tarn Dub, on the far bank of the river which, all initiative spent, it gently feeds along a surface channel.

Below *The entrance to Diccan Cave*

Alum Pot is a fitting end to this chapter on Ingleborough, but it is not to be inferred that the words and photographs adequately describe the manifold attractions of this wonderful mountain; literally they only touch the surface and do not probe the dark secrets beneath.

The band of limestone continues north from Alum Pot on the same contour, the severe Washfold Pot being reached in half a mile, and then curves around the end of Park Fell potholes to complete the encirclement of the mountain at Chapel-le-Dale.

Alum Pot

Amongst the various surface openings in this area, there is one, not far from Alum Pot, that can be recommended to walkers who would like to test their nerves in the darkness and silence of the underworld and, with a torch, may safely do so without encountering perils. This is friendly Borrins Moor Cave and is most easily located by following Alum Pot Beck upstream from Alum Pot to the point where it passes through a gap in the field wall. From this point, a walk west-north-west across the open moor should disclose the entrance in a green hollow: it should be identified exactly (*see* photograph), there being other less welcoming openings nearby. The entrance, attained by a scramble over a boulder, immediately opens into a straight passage with a high roof providing very easy walking for 250 yards; then the roof level drops and further progress is possible only by crawling. This is the place to turn back; the cave continues further for almost a mile but is definitely not for beginners. Even after this short apprenticeship, it is refreshing to return to daylight and safety.

The entrance to Borrins Moor Cave

I conclude this survey of Ingleborough with the same reluctance I feel when leaving the mountain after a day spent in its company, aware that I have failed to do justice to an old friend. Ingleborough is not the highest mountain in the country, as was once thought, but no other can equal its fascination. Someday its proud summit may collapse into its hollow base as erosion continues inexorably. But not yet awhile.

A chapter is not enough to describe this fine mountain. It deserves a book to itself, and a fat volume it would be when all its innermost secrets are known. We can count ourselves fortunate in having Ingleborough in our midst, always there, always waiting for us, always welcoming.

See you again, old pal.

8 NORBER AND MOUGHTON

INGLEBOROUGH IS STURDILY buttressed in the north by Simon Fell and Park Fell, but in the west and east its slopes quickly decline to valley level. In the south-east corner of the massif, however, this fall is interrupted by other heights of sufficient stature and character to be classed not merely as foothills but as separate entities deserving individual attention: of these, Norber and Moughton, enclosing between them the lonely valley of Crummackdale, display features of unusual interest.

The road leading into the pleasant village of Austwick branches from the A65 and at a fork at the north end of the village a left turn, unsignposted, climbs through a leafy avenue into Crummackdale, reaching open country where it is crossed by an unsurfaced lane coming from Clapham. Turn left along this lane; a signpost points the way to Norber, a long limestone ridge forming the north-western skyline. The footpath thereto, at first uneventful, soon mounts a small scar and passes alongside a wall bordering a tilted shelf covered by a scattering of boulders, unremarkable at a glance but having in their midst several amazingly perched on slender pedestals of limestone.

These are the Norber Boulders.

The Norber Boulders are erratics, having no right by birth to be in the place where they are now found. They are strays, having been carried here by the glacier that once occupied Crummackdale as it retreated at the end of the Ice Age, scouring the ground as it departed and bringing down the boulders from their place of origin higher in the valley. Two clues indicate that these boulders are alien to the immediate landscape: they are of darker Silurian rock

Austwick

which contrasts with the white carboniferous limestone on which they have come to rest. Being harder and more durable, they also have withstood the elements over the many centuries that have passed since their arrival, while their softer plinths have been eroded by wind and rain and frost, leaving unaffected only those parts actually under the 'umbrella' protection of the boulders above. However, many of these supports have been eroded by the weather to slender pedestals which, someday in the future, will collapse and unbalance their heavy loads. These supporting stems are about 12 inches tall and indicate the measure of erosion that has taken place in the limestone platforms since their foreign visitors settled upon them. Norber's giant mushrooms have to be seen to be believed.

Above *Norber boulders*
Below *Norber boulder field*

From a stile in the top corner of the enclosure containing the boulders a short climb brings the summit ridge of Norber underfoot and a glorious view over Clapham Bottoms to Ingleborough, from the highest of many cairns at 1320 feet.

Car owners whose main concern is to return to their parked vehicles will need to retrace their steps exactly to avoid steep cliffs at the south end, but others with no such inhibitions can extend the walk, and enjoy doing so, by following the crest of the ridge northwards until meeting the path coming up from Clapham Bottoms bound for Selside, here turning down east to join another path to Selside, this continuing the road along Crummackdale from Austwick. Before turning south to Crummack Farm, cross the moor east to the stream descending in a series of minor waterfalls from the large resurgence at Austwick Beck Head, where all the streams disappearing in the Allotment area on Ingleborough return to daylight.

South of Crummack Farm an alternative and more attractive route of return to Austwick is offered, for pedestrians only, by a lane turning left from the Crummackdale road and appropriately named Moughton Lane, the huge scarred slopes of Moughton being directly ahead. At a T-junction, White Stone Lane leads to the right into the secluded hamlet of Wharfe, Austwick then being a mile further on.

The summit of Norber, looking to Ingleborough

Walkers who wish to combine the ascents of both Norber and Moughton in a single expedition may do so: upon arriving at the T-junction with Norber already conquered, the route of ascent of Moughton from Wharfe should be joined.

Wharfe is a quiet little community that offers no inducements to passersby to disturb its tranquillity. The road giving access to it, branching from the Austwick—Helwith Bridge road, is marked 'Private' and there are no promises of accommodation or refreshments. Hidden in a bower of trees at the southern base of Moughton, the tiny colony of mature and mellowed buildings blends in harmony with the natural environment. It presents a scene of rural contentment, a delectable backwater remote and undisturbed by pressures of the world outside. Wharfe is omitted from mention in official guides to the district and doesn't mind at all.

Above *Crummack Farm, looking to Moughton*
Below *Wharfe*

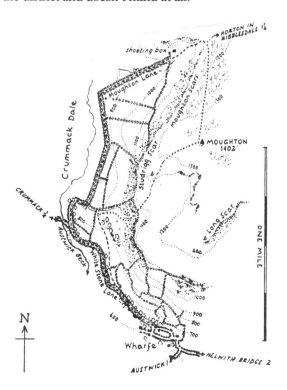

The dry waterfall

The byroad into Wharfe continues as White Stone Lane, for travellers on foot only, and curves around the western base of Moughton amongst evidences on the valley floor of glacial pressures in the underlying rocks, here mainly of shales, slates and gritstone. Beyond the junction with the lane from Crummack, the lane climbs gradually to the ridge at the north end of Moughton, shortly becoming a path. Hereabouts can be found, in quarry spoil, the fine-grained whetstone once transported for use in steel manufacture. Much more likely to attract attention, however, is the rim of cliffs that abruptly ends the approach to the ridge, these dipping to a hollow from which a waterfall once poured in ages past; today, a petrified silence grips the scene.

Above the dry waterfall, the path continues to Horton in Ribblesdale but is left for an easy traverse south along the ridge, passing extensive areas of limestone pavement.

Seen from the A65, the top of Moughton appears unusually flat and dead level for over half a mile. This impression is borne out on close acquaintance, there being little variation in contour on the wide top. The highest inches, however, are not in doubt, the Ordnance Survey having identified the spot by erecting a triangulation column at 1402 feet.

Norber has achieved fame in geological circles by its display of erratic boulders, and Moughton, not to

Moughton's limestone pavement

be outdone, exhibits examples, no less interesting, of unconformity in its rock structures. This is especially evident on the steep edge of Moughton Nab overlooking Helwith Bridge; here, along an easy terrace, there are exposed to view limestone strata, horizontally fissured, resting on low cliffs of vertically fissured Silurian rock.

Descents from Moughton need care in misty conditions. There are no paths on the broad top, which is ringed by scars, and no landmarks other than the Ordnance column to set direction. A direct descent to Wharfe can be made, as indicated by the dotted line on the map, by walking west from the column to the edge of the escarpment and following this south until a breach occurs to permit a passage down the slope to a path that joins White Stone Lane near the hamlet. Cause no damage: there is no official right of way.

Above *Unconformity, Moughton Nab*
Below *The summit of Moughton, looking to Penyghent*

9 UPPER RIBBLESDALE

PASSENGERS LEAVING SETTLE on the railway to Carlisle are usually agog with excitement, this line being acknowledged as scenically the finest in the country. For a few miles initially their anticipation of a beautiful journey is confirmed by lovely surroundings of pastures and woodland as the train passes up the valley of the Ribble with the river in close attendance and friendly green hills rising on both sides of the track. Soon they become aware that the train is engaged on a steady climb, this section being popularly known as the Long Drag; beyond Horton in Ribblesdale Station interest tends to flag a little as the outlook from the windows becomes more austere on the pull up to Ribblehead. On the west side, Ingleborough is a shadowy giant revealing none of the many wonders that attract its legions of pilgrims; and to the east, green slopes rise with little incident to dark moors forming a distant skyline. This eastern aspect is pleasant but, apart from occasional glimpses of the river, promises nothing that warrants close attention.

As elsewhere in limestone country, appearances deceive. The bland slopes bordering and beyond the river, innocuous when seen from the train, abound in hidden secrets that yield to discovery only after a search for them. There are secluded ravines of ferns and flowers bridged by natural arches, waterfalls that plunge into abysmal depths, caves that thread intricate passages below the surface of the ground, cliffs and escarpments that gleam virgin white in the sunshine, streams that dance happily and suddenly disappear. . . . I count Upper Ribblesdale amongst my favourite places on earth. Here imagination catches glimpses of witches and fairies. Especially fairies.

Horton in Ribblesdale is the springboard for explorations in this area. Two roads leave the north end of the village, both on the east side of the river. One is a no-through motor road, the other an ancient cart track; they diverge immediately and then proceed north roughly parallel and half a mile apart. Both lead to the promised land and after three miles can be linked by a path, thus offering a circular walk which, if adopted, makes the use of a car an inconvenience. It is advisable to do the tour anti-clockwise, starting along the cart track thus saving the smooth tarmac for tired legs at the end of the day. Boots are the best footgear on rough terrain and a torch is essential if the intention is to peep or venture into the caves that will be seen en route. Lack of a camera will be regretted.

Here in North Ribblesdale, given fine weather, are all the ingredients for a splendid day of mild adventure. Beautiful scenery is not on the agenda, much of the landscape being barren and unfriendly. But the journey, which coincides in part with the Pennine Way, will remain etched in the memory.

Upper Ribblesdale has long been a magnet for experienced cavers, potholers and geologists. Simple walkers and amateur explorers can share the surface delights but not the underground thrills of discovery.

The cart track, enclosed by walls and known locally as Harber Scar Lane, climbs gradually and uneventfully along the side of Harber Scar and then, quite suddenly and unexpectedly, the traveller upon it is confronted by a scene that demands instant attention and dispels all else from his mind. The track ahead crosses a natural bridge between sinister cavities without the protection of a parapet. A stream comes down on the east side and disappears into a cave entrance admitting to a passage below the track where, on the west side, it is joined underground from an alternative pothole entrance. These are Sell Gill Holes, first explored in Victorian times. Vertical pitches descend 250 feet to an immense cavern, second in dimensions only to the chamber in Gaping Gill. Many caves are located only after diligent search. Sell Gill saves you the trouble. Here is a fantasy in limestone that cannot be missed.

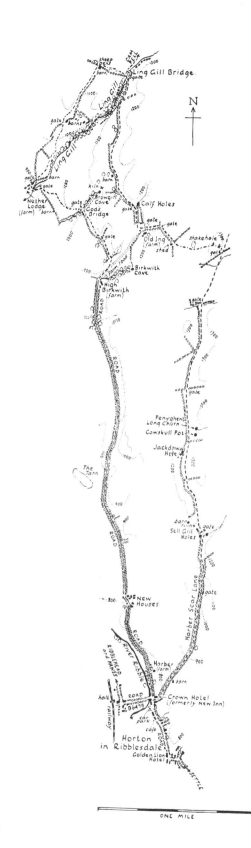

Above *The road leaving Horton for High Birkwith*
Below *The cart track leading to Sell Gill*

Sell Gill Holes

The track continues north beyond Sell Gill, alongside a line of shakeholes that indicate a collapse of the underlying limestone. A walled enclosure on the left, with trees, soon appears, concealing the large and impressive opening of Jackdaw Hole, 130 feet deep, and across the moor north-east from this point is the even deeper shaft of Penyghent Long Churn, admitting a stream: both holes can be inspected from safe stances on the surface but should not be approached too closely. Other minor fissures will be noticed as the track goes forward, soon to be crossed by the Three Peaks route, which heads away to the left at a tangent. A short mile further on, a gate in a wall to the left gives access to the isolated farmhouse of Old Ing.

Penyghent Long Churn Pot

Old Ing

Old Ing is the apex of the circular walk and here a decision must be taken, either to return at once to Horton in Ribblesdale by way of the motor road, in which case the farm access road descending south-west to High Birkwith should be followed, turning aside to see Birkwith Cave on the left; or preferably, if the legs are willing, a recommended three-mile detour north will yield further surprises and delights.

An easy cart track heads north and in five minutes arrives at Dry Laithe Cave, commonly known as Calf Holes, where a stream coming down on the right disappears in a rash of rocks and passes into a cave under the track. The place of its emergence into daylight will be seen on the return journey.

Calf Holes

The track goes on as a pleasant lane beyond Calf Holes, coming alongside a belt of trees on the left and arriving after a mile at the sixteenth-century Ling Gill Bridge, a modest structure with a tablet built into the parapet giving the information that it was repaired in 1765 at the expense of the inhabitants of the West Riding. The bridge was constructed of gritstone from the bed of Cam Beck, which it spans, and marks a transition from the limestone of Upper Ribblesdale to the coarser rocks of the Pennines. The track continues north climbing to Cam End as part of the Pennine Way, but for walkers based at Horton this is the place to turn back.

Ling Gill Bridge

Before returning, a look down into the tremendous ravine of Ling Gill below the bridge will reveal a most impressive scene, the beck hurrying along a bouldery bed fringed by trees and cliffs on its way to join the Ribble; several minor caves have been found and explored along its banks but the rough terrain is a deterrent to walkers who prefer to travel sedately. Ling Gill is better enjoyed from its outer rim than from its confines.

Ling Gill

Browgill Cave

Returning along the track, a gate in the wall on the right near a barn, 200 yards short of Calf Holes, admits to a sloping field with a sharp descent after passing a limekiln, to Browgill Cave; the stream which issues from there is the one that disappears into Calf Holes. Browgill Cave is friendly to novices, and provides an easy passage into its interior. Rough ground needs care for 70 yards until the roof drops and further progress is possible only by crawling; here amateur explorers must turn back to daylight, lack of experience denying them further access into a waterfall chamber and eventual emergence at Calf Holes.

The stream may be followed down the field to a lateral path which crosses it by yet another God's Bridge, a stone arch formed by nature. The path to the left leads to the Old Ing farm access road above High Birkwith. Nearby at this point and reached by going up the road to a path bearing right, is the dark and intimidating Birkwith Cave, a strong debouching stream denying easy access.

God's Bridge, Browgill

This stream passes down a wooded ravine with no access, steps having to be retraced to the Old Ing road. From here, a turn down to the left leads to High Birkwith and then two miles of uneventful tarmac, heading south to the starting point of the walk at Horton. Midway, over the wall bordering the road on the right, will be seen at close range The Tarn with the Ribble beyond and Ingleborough forming a massive background.

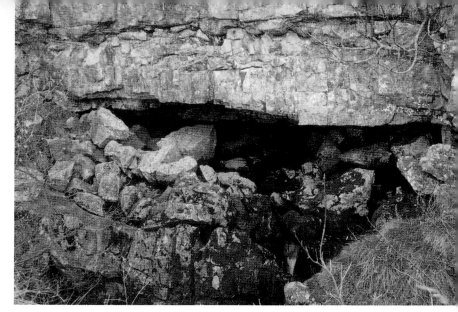

Above *Birkwith Cave*
Below *The tarn on the High Birkwith road*

THORNS GILL

Thorns Gill carries the infant Ribble down from its birthplace on Newby Head Moss and follows a course parallel to a section of the B6255 road between Ingleton and Hawes. It is, however, unseen and unsuspected by travellers along the road and its charms are known only by a relative few who have discovered its existence during their wanderings in the area. There is currently an unresolved contention by the landowners that there is no public right of way along the gill, and they are probably right; the County Council, called upon to settle the issue, is faced with evidence from myself and others that the gill has been visited without challenge since Victorian times. In the meantime, and possibly in the future, permission should be sought at Far Gearstones Farm nearby. There is also a proposal afoot to re-route the Three Peaks Walk across Thorns Gill, which I hope will be rejected. Thorns Gill is too precious to suffer damage by boots racing against the clock.

From Gearstones an undisputed path goes down to a footbridge over the stream, here known as Gayle Beck. Thorns Gill is downstream from the bridge and on the north bank after a minute's walk is seen the entrance to Holme Hill Cave, formerly defended by an iron gate giving access to lengthy underground passages. Further down the gill, on a high bank on the south side and at the base of a low cliff, is the opening of Capnut (or Katnot) Cave where a roomy passage can be followed without encountering difficulties other than darkness for a hundred yards before returning to daylight. Experts (only) can penetrate here a third of a mile. It was in this cave that I came across another example of Yorkshire wit: revealed in the light of a torch was a daubed inscription on the wall of the cave, 'J. CAESAR B.C. 44'.

Spanning the tree-lined gorge of the stream below Capnut Cave is the picturesque stone arch of the narrow Thorns Gill Bridge, a lovely place for a halt and a gem for the camera and the canvas. Here man and nature have achieved perfect harmony. Direct access to this beautiful scene can be gained, probably unlawfully, from a field gate on the road above: for peace of mind to supplement the peace of the bridge, get permission from Gearstones Farm to visit.

Holme Hill Cave   *Capnut Cave*

Thorns Gill Bridge

Below the bridge, the stream, so far well behaved, vanishes in a fit of petulance into Thorns Gill Cave on its north bank, the interior being out of bounds to all but experienced cavers. When it returns to surface daylight, it flows quietly down to valley level at Ribblehead; here it adopts the name of River Ribble and turns south on its long journey to Preston and the Irish Sea.

RIBBLEHEAD

East of the Ribblehead railway viaduct and almost in its evening shadow is the desolate moorland of Batty Green, an inhospitable tract of rough ground without distinguishing landmarks and apparently devoid of interest except to grazing sheep, with nothing to earn a second glance by motorists on the Ingleton—Hawes road alongside. A thousand feet above sea level and defenceless against extremes of weather, it is a wilderness where nobody would choose to live.

Yet in the 1870s, Batty Green was the centre of animated activity. Here was a shanty town of huts housing the hundreds of men engaged in the construction of the viaduct, living in discomfort with their wives and children, exposed to the elements and suffering a toll of casualties resulting from hardship and adverse conditions. These rough men did a magnificent job, creating a work of art with primitive tools and equipment – but at a heavy price in human lives. The work finished, the dead buried and the site cleared, Batty Green reverted to a sullen silence broken now only by the occasional passage of trains, the rhythmic pulse of their wheels seeming to sound a requiem for those who perished.

This barren and featureless area offers no promise of adventure, yet within a mile of the viaduct the unlikely terrain yields the secrets of a score of caves and potholes to those who search and succeed in locating them: some are easy, some are difficult, some are dangerous, and most remain shyly hidden.

Batty Wife Cave is in a different category, having no pretensions to shyness nor modesty; indeed, it thrusts itself upon the notice of passersby on the road just below the Station Inn on the north side, where a channel of pebbles emerges from a low entrance half-choked by stones and normally dry. The cave is ten yards long with a low roof and has nothing of interest, its only merit being as a safe refuge from rain and wind.

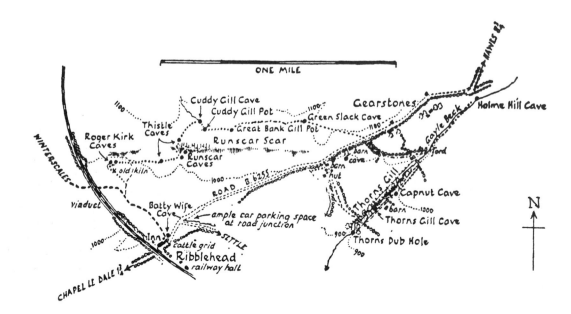

Roger Kirk Cave

Cuddy Gill Pot

A good cart track, navigable by cars, leaves the road near Batty Wife Cave and passes under the viaduct bound for Gunnerside. The first section of this, before reaching the viaduct, is a springboard for a circular tour of the Batty Green Holes, visiting in particular Roger Kirk Cave, Cuddy Gill Pot and Runscar Caves before returning to the road. Many more, including some not shown on the map, will probably be seen en route. The safe rule for amateur explorers is, having located a cave, not to enter it beyond the limits of daylight and then only with a torch and a companion; some of the interiors drop sharply in vertical pitches and shafts.

Enthusiasts who are both cave spotters and train spotters will enjoy Batty Green; others not so addicted will probably not, the area being pathless and rough underfoot and lacking the beauty of other parts of the region.

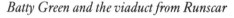

Batty Green and the viaduct from Runscar

10 PENYGHENT AND FOUNTAINS FELL

PENYGHENT IS THE eastern point of the triangle formed by the Three Peaks and, at 2273 feet, the lowest in terms of altitude. It rises starkly above Horton in Ribblesdale, this being its finest aspect. North-east of the summit, high ground continues for some miles over the less obtrusive Plover Hill before descending to valley level at the head of Littondale. Penyghent is visited on the Pennine Way marathon and is the highest ground so far reached on the journey from the start at Edale, and usually the first objective on the Three Peaks Walk. It is also a compelling attraction for visitors based on Ribblesdale, and the amount of foot traffic so generated has caused severe erosion of the few paths on the soft peat of the upper slopes, the damage being only partially remedied by the placing of duckboards and fencing laid across the path most commonly in use.

When I first climbed Penyghent the path could barely be discerned in the tough grass; today it has the dimensions of a road, its misuse being largely due to parties walking abreast and chattering instead of walking sedately in single file as all should do on narrow paths. On a recent visit, I witnessed a group of thirty school children advancing like an army, but without military discipline, straying over the verges of the path, having great fun kicking the surface stones around, shattering the silence with their shouts and generally out of the control of their accompanying teachers. Classroom codes of conduct and obedience should be applied equally on outside excursions. Blessed be the solitary walker.

Penyghent has many interesting features, some of them spectacular, which are almost exclusively centred on the western slopes above Horton in Ribblesdale. As with Ingleborough, the higher slopes and the summit are typical Pennine grits covered by peat and rough grass with the exception, particularly on Penyghent, of a ring of limestone cliffs; these form a vertical garden of the lovely purple saxifrage, which sadly in recent years has been decimated by flaking cliff faces. Like Ingleborough, too, the top one thousand feet of the mountain are supported on an immense plinth of carboniferous limestone. The point of fusion is emphasised along an even contour where water draining from the surface above has carved and fissured the softer rock below in a slow process ever since the mountain took shape. Ages of erosion have contributed to the formation of innumerable underground passages that penetrate hundreds of feet into the earth from rifts and shafts on the surface, their exploration providing adventure for a growing number of caving enthusiasts.

On other sides of Penyghent, the landscape is Pennine in appearance and character, wild and untamed slopes used as sheep pastures declining to occasional farmsteads and settlements in the surrounding sheltered valleys. But it is in the west that the mountain's greatest attractions are to be found, among them the largest natural surface opening in the country, the deepest pothole, a tall and slender pinnacle that has miraculously survived the ravages of the ages and, at valley level, twin caves of debouchure from which issue the streams that sink out of sight higher on the mountain side.

The Ordnance Survey persist in giving this fine mountain a hyphenated name, Pen-y-Ghent, a distinction commonly accepted as a mark of superior status although not observed in conversation nor indeed in most written references. But the high class is certainly there.

Penyghent from Brackenbottom Scar

Ascent from Horton in Ribblesdale

Two routes of ascent from Horton in Ribblesdale are commonly in use, popular among visitors not engaged in either of the long distance walks that leave the village: the first follows Horton Scar Lane between confining walls to the open moorland, and the other, more direct and adopted by Three Peaks walkers, prefers field paths rising beyond the suburb of Brackenbottom and ends more steeply. Pennine Wayfarers travelling south to north approach from the neighbouring Fountains Fell, crossing the Helwith Bridge—Halton Gill road to make a direct assault therefrom.

Horton Scar Lane rises gradually from the village, with improving views fore and aft, and ends at an old shooting hut where the path to Penyghent turns to the right across open ground. From the hut, a short detour along a path continuing the line of approach leads in minutes to the huge opening of Hull Pot, a steep-sided crater 100 yards long, 20 yards wide, 60 feet deep and partly collapsed at the north end. This spectacular hole in the ground is fed by a stream coming in from the east which, in normal weather, sinks in its bed before reaching the lip of the chasm to reappear under the bouldery floor but, after heavy rain, persists to the edge and tumbles into the depths as a fine waterfall. Only once in many visits have I witnessed this, and on very rare occasions following heavy floods, the hole has filled completely with water. At the bottom of the hole, unseen from above, the stream reappears in subterranean passages.

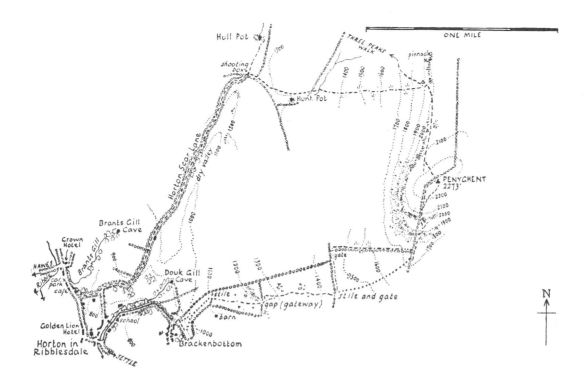

Hull Pot

1700

THREE PEAKS WALK

1400 1500 1600 pinnacle

ONE MILE

shooting box

Hunt. Pot

1700 1800 1900 2000

2100

Horton Scar Lane

dry valley 1100 1200 1300

1000

Brants Gill Cave

Crown Hotel

HAWES

Ribblesdale

car park cafe

Douk Gill Cave

800

900

PENYGHENT 2273'

2200

2100

2000 1900

1800 1700

1100 1200 1300

gate

1500

stile

gap (gateway)

barn

stile and gate

Golden Lion Hotel

school

(PROW)

1000

Horton in Ribblesdale

SETTLE

Brackenbottom

N

Opposite *Horton Scar Lane*

Below *Hull Pot*

Hunt Pot

Five minutes after leaving the shooting hut on the path to the summit, a short detour over the rough moor to the right arrives suddenly on the brink of Hunt Pot, occupying a large hollow where a stream falls into an evil slit in the floor. The sides of the hollow can be negotiated with care but it is not advised to inspect the hole too closely, this being a vertical shaft 200 feet in depth.

Underground streams do not always follow the course one might expect from a study of the surface topography and this is illustrated by the water vanishing into Hull Pot and Hunt Pot which reappears down in the valley at resurgences in cave openings at Brants Gill and Douk Gill. Chemical tests have proved that their channels cross at different levels somewhere during their descent from the moor above.

Returning to the path, the way forward makes a beeline for the line of cliffs ahead and far above. Interest flags as the limestone features are left behind, being succeeded by a zone of grits and shales covered by tough grass and peat; this is churned to a slippery morass by countless boots. Attempts have been made in some sections of the path to restore a firm footing by placing boards and chestnut paling across the parts most affected. Arrival at the base of the cliffs is a relief. Here the path inclines sharply right, but a detour below the crags to the left soon brings into view a remarkable slender pinnacle detached by erosion from the face of the cliff and some 60 feet in height.

The rock hereabouts, an intrusive band of limestone, was until recently the habitat of the beautiful purple saxifrage which occupied the niches and cracks in the face of the cliffs and every April provided a wonderful display. On a recent visit, alas, I was dismayed to find that the face of the cliff had disintegrated further, stripping off the plants, which were buried in new debris along the base. Only a few survivors could be found.

Brants Gill Cave

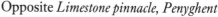

Opposite *Limestone pinnacle, Penyghent*

The summit of Penyghent

The final section of the path traverses firmer ground, rising at an even gradient and passing above the cliffs and ends, with the summit obviously near, in a rash of beelines to the stile in the ridge wall. The cairn is then only a few paces beyond with an Ordnance column alongside. The reward for the effort of getting there is an extensive panorama, best seen and appreciated by a perambulation of the rim of the summit cliffs.

Ingleborough from the summit of Penyghent

Above *Horton in Ribblesdale church and Penyghent*
Below *The lane to Brackenbottom*

Ascent from Brackenbottom

A less frequented but more direct approach leaves the valley at Brackenbottom, reached in half a mile by a pleasant lane starting behind Horton's church. This is the route followed by Three Peaks walkers who are always in a hurry, but is less likely to be preferred by others not racing against the clock to the more popular way along Horton Scar Lane.

A field path climbs gradually through walled pastures provided with stiles and gates, and reaches the substantial intake wall along the western side of the mountain on the 1000-ft contour. Over this the slope ahead can be followed to join the south ridge wall heading straight for the summit.

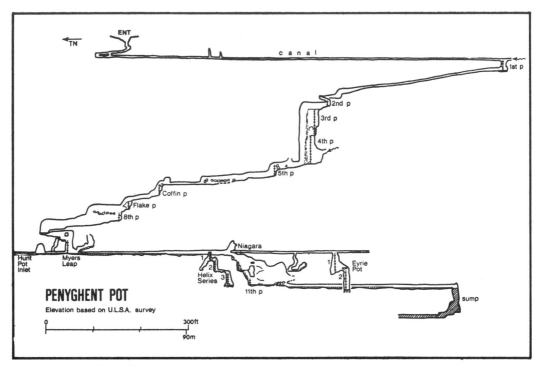

PENYGHENT POT

Elevation based on U.L.S.A. survey

From Northern Caves (Volume 2) © Dalesman Publishing Co Ltd.

Walkers with time to spare can conveniently visit the entrance to the notorious Penyghent Pot by following the top side of the intake wall to the left, crossing another wall that goes uphill at a tangent and arriving in five more minutes at a stream sink east of the wall. Here an insignificant opening amongst boulders, seemingly innocent of the terrors to which it leads, is the gateway to the deepest, most dangerous and intricate of all potholes. This is Penyghent Pot, a succession of long wet crawls and eight vertical pitches that lead down into the earth to a depth of almost 600 feet at a final sump where divers have been unable to proceed further. This is an arduous expedition, encumbered by the ladders and lifelines that have to be pushed along the narrow passages. Consequently, the pot has an unenviable record of casualties and rescues, many occasioned when members of a party, having struggled to get down to the lower reaches, find themselves too exhausted to return to the surface. Penyghent Pot is for tough men only.

Returning from Penyghent Pot, the tangent wall can be followed alongside to its junction with the south ridge wall, here joining the route of the Pennine Way and Three Peaks walkers for the final steepening slope through a breach in the summit cliffs to the easy top beyond.

The summit cliffs

Dale Head Farm

Churn Milk Hole

Ascent from Stainforth

A quiet minor motor road leaves Ribblesdale at Stainforth and climbs steadily to the pass between Penyghent and Fountains Fell before descending into Littondale. Car owners can save the uphill trudge to an access road leading to Dale Head Farm on the left, the Pennine Way here joining after descending from Fountains Fell. Dale Head is isolated but not lonely; apart from the Pennine Way walkers who pass its doors on most days of the year, it is a centre of caving and potholing activity. The buildings have survived not only the storms of centuries but the risk of subsidence: the area around is a network of underground passages opening to the surface, among them Dale Head Pot, a twin to Penyghent Pot in depth, danger and difficulty. A track goes on beyond the farmhouse and at the large shakehole of Churn Milk Hole turns due north to come alongside the south ridge wall for the final scramble to the top.

The south ridge, Penyghent

FOUNTAINS FELL

Fountains Fell, a close neighbour of Penyghent, is excluded from the august company of the Three Peaks, not because of any shortcomings in elevation, the summit at 2191 feet being little lower than that of Penyghent, but presumably because the sprawling top quite lacks the distinctive shape of the others. Hurt pride was salvaged, however, when the Pennine Way elected to give patronage to the misfit, three miles of the route being devoted to a traverse of the fell.

Stone men on the summit

The name derives from Fountains Abbey, once the landowner here. The extensive top of the fell was not always the barren desolation it is today: in days long gone, it was a centre of mining activity; traces remain in a number of coal pits, their shafts now filled in, and remnants of colliery buildings. Cairns are plentiful, some serving to indicate the path across the top, others acting as landmarks; on the northern edge are two handsome stone men. This sad scene of abandoned enterprise is graced somewhat by a large tarn, but little else relieves the desolation all around. Industrial archaeologists may find relics of interest but there is little inducement for others to linger. The presence of coal measures indicates an absence of limestone: millstone grit is the bedrock of the higher parts of Fountains Fell.

But limestone enthusiasts are generously catered for at mid-height on the southern flank. A track leaves the road opposite the access to Dale Head Farm and in a short mile reaches an area in complete contrast to the shaggy and uninteresting slopes above. Here, within a square half-mile, fifty holes pierce the ground, some simple shakeholes, others penetrating the ground for hundreds of feet and providing major expeditions of great severity. Sheep need to tread warily in this tortured landscape. So should its visitors.

Penyghent from Fountains Fell

Gingling Hole   *Magnetometer Pot*

Excitement erupts as the track enters an area of disturbed ground where two stream channels, choked by boulders, come down from the moors, their waters vanishing into the depths of Gingling Sink. Nearby is a classic pothole, Gingling Hole, opening in a shakehole and dropping over 500 feet into the earth in a series of passages and shafts: this is one of the major potholes in the district. And there are others no less severe in the immediate vicinity: Echo Pot, Hammer Pot and Magnetometer Pot all offer arduous expeditions into the nether regions. There is danger from unstable rock: on my first visit, Coates Cavern could be inspected in safety but the walls have since collapsed into a heap of boulders.

In a pasture adjacent to the main concentration of potholes is a remarkable proliferation of minor holes in a tight group, twenty-three in all. Cavers are usually quick to fit appropriate names to their discoveries but here were at a loss for ideas and they are indicated by numbers, 1 to 23, in caving guidebooks. The only habitation hereabouts at least has a suitable name: Rough Close exactly fits this patch of limestone on the side of Fountains Fell.

11 THE ENVIRONS OF SETTLE

I HAVE HAD AN affection for Settle ever since my first visit as a young man. In those early days, before the war, travel was a luxury few could afford: most people in the industrial towns of Lancashire, and no doubt elsewhere, were penned in their homes by near-poverty with few opportunities to escape. But occasionally cheap excursion trains ran day-trips up the Ribble valley, and when funds permitted I was a passenger, eager to see new landscapes and never in a hurry to return.

Settle was another world. I loved to wander along the narrow streets and alleys, to look at the Shambles and the Folly and other quaint buildings that added a medieval atmosphere to the little town and have a bite to eat at the Naked Man café before making my way reluctantly back to the railway station and home. These were the days before traffic lights and yellow lines and car parks, the streets were not burdened by overmuch traffic and the residents were kind, helpful and unhurried.

But most of all, when time permitted, I liked to scramble to the top of the limestone cliff of Castleberg overlooking and dominating the town and sit by its proud flagpole and see Settle as a bird sees it.

Settle charmed me as a youth, and still does as an old man, but a greater attraction for me has always been the close surround of green hills in which the town nestles. Wave after wave of rolling emerald uplands with white necklaces of limestone scars stretching to distant horizons. On these lovely heights, the close-cropped turf is a joy to tread, thanks to the custodian sheep, and walking is a pleasure. In the course of many years, with more time and money available, I wandered everywhere on these hills, finding surprises and delights unsuspected from the valley, treasures worth the seeking. All this and Settle too!

Settle, from Castleberg

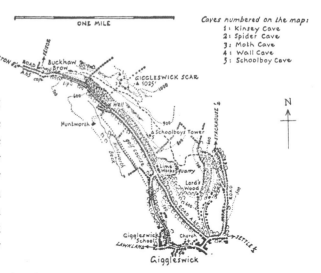

Caves numbered on the map:
1 : Kinsey Cave
2 : Spider Cave
3 : Moth Cave
4 : Wall Cave
5 : Schoolboy Cave

GIGGLESWICK SCAR

Settle has recently been bypassed, a re-routed A65 skirting the town to the south and west, and the former highway over Buckhaw Brow, long a scourge to cyclists and drivers of vehicles past their best, may now be walked with less danger of annihilation by fast-moving traffic. Today it may be trodden in relative safety as part of a short circular walk from Settle introducing the ancient parish of Giggleswick and the limestone scar overlooking the many interesting buildings in this little community.

The road leaves Settle over the bridge across the River Ribble and climbs to the outskirts of Giggleswick. Here a diversion down to the left traverses the main street of that village, passing the parish church of St Alkelda and, amongst noble trees, the well-known Giggleswick public school; this was founded five centuries ago, and its fame enhanced in 1927 when the then Astronomer Royal selected the school observatory as his viewpoint for observing the eclipse of the sun. A conspicuous landmark here is the green-domed school chapel.

Giggleswick's parish church   *The school chapel*

The main road is rejoined beyond the school opposite a huge quarry and followed to the left past a golf course, not the best in the country, and the shallow valley of Huntworth Beck. A tarn drained here in 1837 brought to light a canoe considered by experts to be 2000 years old. But of more immediate interest and soon reached is the roadside Ebbing and Flowing Well; the curious rise and fall of its waters, a phenomenon first recorded in 1612, has attracted the attention of passersby ever since, the erratic movement of its waters thought to be caused by a natural double siphon. In many visits, I have never seen it operating, the well being choked by leaves and tourist litter, but two correspondents at different times in recent years have reported to me that they have witnessed it functioning as promised.

Now the road starts its long climb up Buckhaw Brow, a third lane having been added for fast traffic before the bypass of Settle was planned. Escape from the tarmac is provided by a gate in the north roadside wall, but a continuation to the top of the brow is well worth the extra effort; the retrospective view from there of Giggleswick Scar high on the left, the rich woodland below it, the sweet valley going down to join the Ribble and the green background of hills makes a beautiful picture.

The view east from Buckhaw Brow

Above *Schoolboys Tower*

Below *Penyghent from Giggleswick Scar*

From the gate in the wall below the top of Buckhaw Brow, a path rises diagonally to a natural terrace between the scar and the woodland below. Along here is a succession of caves in the base of the cliffs, short and simple openings excellent for a first apprenticeship in cave exploration. Evidences of early British occupation have been found in these caves and Kinsey Cave produced the skull of a bear. A notable landmark as the walk proceeds is Schoolboys Tower, a large cairn of stones, presumably the work of a past generation of boys from Giggleswick School, and nearby a splendid prospect of Ribblesdale backed by Penyghent comes into view.

Above *Giggleswick Quarry*
Right *In Lord's Wood*

Care is needed in descending from Giggleswick Scar in bad weather. The huge quarry at the south-eastern end of the scar seems to get larger every time I pass, a tremendous hollow having been scooped out of the fellside with vertical walls hundreds of feet high, and unless the quarry owners are restrained by planning prohibitions, future visitors will see a Giggleswick Scar much shrivelled in size and humiliated by its use as road material.

In clear weather, the dangers of the quarry are palpably obvious and a path skirts the upper edge and enters Lord's Wood for a pleasant descent to the road half a mile from Settle.

This walk, Settle to Settle, is a pleasant excursion of six miles with not more than a thousand feet of climbing and excelling in lovely views. It is to be hoped that more slices are not cut out of Giggleswick Scar.

Feizor

FEIZOR

Feizor is a small farming community with a few cottages snugly hidden in a shallow fold of the hills, its Norse name suggesting a long occupation. It is reached, but not often by casual visitors who have no business there, by a narrow road branching from the old highway linking Clapham and Settle, discarded and bypassed by a new section of the A65 and now as likely to be frequented by grazing cows on the verges as by cars on the tarmac. And recently the A65 has been re-routed on another bypass to the south, leaving Feizor still more remote and isolated from the pulsating life of the busy world outside its domain. Not that Feizor minds its isolation. It has been bypassed by time too. Gates across the access road defend its privacy; the old pump and drinking trough still remain as symbols of a life that has not accepted change. Lip service was paid to progress by the road being surfaced; otherwise Feizor can manage quite well, thank you, and is well content to be left alone. There are no signs of welcome. Strangers here are intruders.

Feizor may also be approached from the top of Buckhaw Brow where a wicket gate admits to a footpath that rises through a breach in the limestone scars bordering the road and then heads directly for the hamlet across high and open pastures. Here, out of the sight and noise of traffic, the surrounding landscape of green hills splashed with white, can be surveyed and, because all is fair to look upon, appreciated and enjoyed. Ahead, across a valley, the summits of Pot Scar and Smearsett Scar top a long limestone ridge, copses and woodlands grace the middle distance, and Ingleborough and Penyghent form impressive backgrounds to a lovely scene.

Feizor is a place for those who travel on their feet, not in cars. There are delightful walks around, most unfrequented. Other footpaths lead to Little Stainforth and Stackhouse, an exhilarating traverse can be made over Pot Scar to the sudden terminus of the ridge at Smearsett Scar, and a short journey back in time can be made to the Celtic Wall.

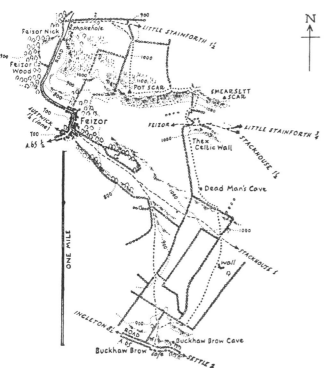

The best expedition from Feizor, a short one, climbs to the stony summit of Pot Scar, from a signpost in the village.

The top of Pot Scar is a desert of stones with large cairns suggesting that other walkers have been here before. The well-defined ridge leads eastwards to its abrupt end on Smearsett Scar, a splendid viewpoint bearing a cairn and a column of the Ordnance Survey. The valley down on the right during this traverse is known locally as the Happy Valley and across it on the hillside is seen the Celtic Wall. The sides of the ridge are rough and the return to Feizor should be made the same way, or the footpath in the valley joined on reaching easier ground.

Below left *The summit of Pot Scar*
Below right *The summit of Smearsett Scar*

THE CELTIC WALL

Settle's recorded history goes back a long way, the first market charter being granted in 1248 but there are evidences of occupation thousands of years before in the dark ages of prehistory, primitive hunting weapons having been found. Excavations in some of the nearby caves have revealed that they were the shelters and cemeteries of species of wild animals long extinct in the country, their unearthed bones having been identified as those of bear, deer and larger animals in early stages of evolution. These relics of a forgotten past were collected, classified and placed on display in a private museum at Townhead, Settle. The museum is now closed and the contents dispersed to other museums.

One notable antiquity, however, remains on its original site, open to the sky and still in pristine condition, having withstood the storms of centuries. This is the Celtic Wall, a substantial structure of blocks of limestone gathered from outcrops in the vicinity, 65 feet in length and 5 feet thick; it is attributed by local historians to the invaders from over the Border, some of whom after many skirmishes with the native Britons made their homes in the district. The purpose of the wall is obscure: it is open ended and did not form part of an enclosure, nor did it mark a boundary. Its strategic position, on the rim of an upland overlooking the Happy Valley, suggests a defensive use, to repel invaders; but this is conjecture and it remains a mystery.

The Celtic Wall can be reached quickly from the Feizor—Stackhouse path, or from the gate at the top of Buckhaw Brow, diverging from the Feizor path to cross a former rifle range and passing Dead Man's Cave, an easy aperture with no hazards – and no human corpses.

The Celtic wall

The stepping stones, Stainforth

STAINFORTH

Stainforth is a pleasant village astride the B6479 three miles north of Settle, well aware of the natural attractions of its surroundings. It caters generously for the many visitors who halt or sojourn there with a choice of hotel and cottage accommodation, a Youth Hostel and ample camping and caravan sites; Stainforth stakes a fair claim to be classed as an inland holiday resort.

A moorland road branches off here and climbs to a pass between Penyghent and Fountains Fell before descending to Littondale and Wharfedale, a scenic route for motorists.

Of more interest to walkers is a lane that rises east from the village for a mile to come alongside a wooded gorge into which plunges the highest waterfall in Ribblesdale, the spectacular Catrigg Force where, in a moment of high drama, Cowside Beck suddenly ends its moorland meanderings and leaps into the depths of a ravine fringed by trees, with ferns and flowers relieving the starkness of the towering cliffs.

On the west bank of the Ribble is the detached outpost of Little Stainforth, which may be reached independently by a riverside walk from Settle. Here is Stainforth Hall, its former quiet isolation fallen victim to an invasion of tents and caravans, an encampment that mars the peace of a very beautiful part of the river but does not detract from its visual delights.

Catrigg Force

The ancient bridge spanning the Ribble at Little Stainforth is the most elegant arch along the course of the river. It was built in the 1670s by local craftsmen on the instructions of the monks of Sawley Abbey who then owned the estate here, and was originally on the packhorse trade route from Lancaster to York. It is now in the care of the National Trust.

Downriver from the bridge is Stainforth Force where the smooth-flowing waters suddenly break free of their restraints and dance excitedly to lower levels in a series of foaming cascades before again resuming a placid course.

Above *Stainforth Bridge*
Below *Stainforth Force*

LANGCLIFFE

A mile north of Settle, adjacent to the B6479 but happily not disturbed by its traffic, Langcliffe arranges itself around a village green and lets the busy world go by. The green in spacious, with proud decorations, the best known being the Big Tree, an ancient sycamore enclosed by a tight fence and ringed by seats; there is a drinking fountain and a war memorial nearby. On the wall of one of the cottages, not to be outdone by Settle's Naked Man, is the effigy of a Naked Woman. The minor road passing through the village climbs amongst limestone scars and outcrops over the hills to the Malham area, providing fine views of Ribblesdale on the way.

Victoria Cave, the largest open cavern in the district, the best known and the most prolific in its yield of prehistoric relics, can be reached from Langcliffe quickly and easily by following the Malham road for half a mile, there taking a cart track on the right. A short walk south alongside the intake wall leads to the escarpment in which the cave will be found amongst lesser openings. Failure to notice it is impossible, a well-trodden path leading up to the gaping entrance 30 feet high and as wide.

The year of discovery is usually stated as 1838, by men hunting foxes, but excavations of its floor have proved beyond doubt that it was known and occupied as a refuge tens of thousands of years ago, successive layers of bones sandwiched between deposits of sediment having been identified as those of animal species long extinct in this country. The relics discovered in this cave as the result of repeated scientific diggings have been prolific, enabling the age of the various specimens to be determined, and in some cases the course of their evolution traced. Darwin would have enjoyed Victoria Cave. It has proved to be a prehistoric museum.

The Big Tree, Langcliffe

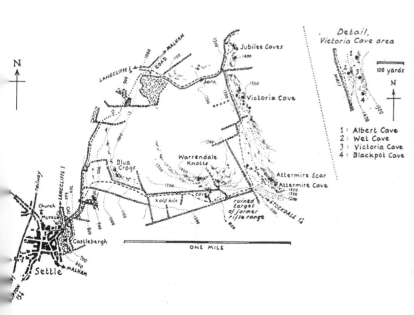

The imposing entrance to Victoria Cave is artificial, the original point of access being an inconspicuous opening to the left which probably accounts for its non-discovery until relatively modern times. Passages lead off the huge interior chamber but these are not for the casual visitor who, in the diffused daylight, must be content to exercise his imagination and picture the scene when the cavern was a pit of darkness occupied by primitive man and animals unknown until Victoria Cave told us their story.

The present artificial entrance to Victoria Cave

Below *the natural entrance*

The walk up to Victoria Cave from Langcliffe can be extended to provide an interesting and very pleasant circular tour if the return is to be made to Settle. By following the wall south along the base of the escarpment for a short mile, the towering cliff of Attermire Scar is reached. This gives an opportunity to look into Attermire Cave which, unusually, opens in the face and not at the base but can be entered along a ledge to the left. Inside, a high passage can be followed for some fifty yards until confronted by difficulties. A feature of almost all the caves along this escarpment is their ease and safety of access, making it a profitable area for the beginner in cave exploration.

Attermire gets its name from the marshy ground below the scar, once a tarn and formerly known as Otters Mere; it was later used as a rifle range.

The shallow valley heading west from the foot of Attermire Scar and passing below the naked cliffs of Warrendale Knotts, offers an easy route of return to Settle on a good path between walls. The path enters Banks Lane, with impressive views over the town and valley, and descends sharly down Constitution Hill to the Market Place.

Above *Attermire Scar and Cave*
Below *Warrendale Knotts*

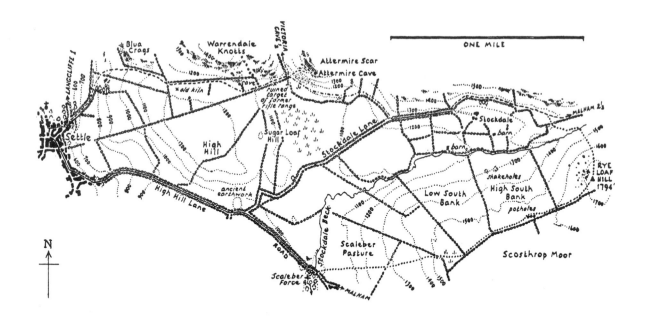

Stockdale Farm and Rye Loaf Hill

STOCKDALE

The motor road from Settle to Malham climbs steeply beyond the last buildings of the town, passing along the side of High Hill to reach open moorland at an elevation of a thousand feet with Attermire Scar rising to the north. At a junction, the access road to Stockdale Farm turns away eastwards for a long mile to the farm, whence a bridleway continues forward to Malham. The valley of Stockdale is bare and has few attractions to delay the average walker passing through but it provides a rich harvest for the caving fraternity who have a choice of a score of holes they can disappear into. The commanding height hereabouts is Rye Loaf Hill, 1794 feet, and the ascent may be made as shown by the dotted line on the map. As there is no path or right of way, it would be prudent to get the farmer's permission before venturing across his pastures.

Summit cairn on Rye Loaf Hill

Below *Scaleber Force*

The summit of Rye Loaf Hill is crowned by a large cairn and enjoys extensive views in all directions, Malhamdale and upper Airedale both being in sight.

A direct return to the Settle—Malham road can be made by following the ridge wall south-west over High South Bank, notable for a profusion of shake-holes, and at its end crossing pastures due west to the road at Scaleber.

Stockdale Beck passes under the road and enters a wooded glen accompanied by a popular path that soon comes alongside Scaleber (pronounced Scallyber) Force, a spectacular waterfall 40 feet high.

The stream here is in a hurry to join the Ribble, but their meeting is delayed by a deflecting ridge that turns the stream south on a parallel course for many miles before easier contours permit a union beyond Long Preston.

12 MALHAMDALE

THE VILLAGE OF MALHAM has long been a weekend target for the people of north Lancashire and the Yorkshire Dales. In the early days before the war, when only the mill-owners had cars, getting there was a problem, the alternatives being a long walk from Gargrave or reliance on an infrequent bus service from Skipton: a visit was a rare treat to be thought about and talked about for days afterwards. Gradually, following the war as the mill folk in the nearby industrial towns enjoyed more leisure time and had more money in their pockets and walkers no longer considered travel in motorcars an indignity, Malham provided a complete escape from their everyday urban environment and visitors arrived in increasing numbers, many in excursion coaches; Malham had its first car park. Then there began to appear in the village a different type of pedestrian, hikers rather than walkers, heavy-booted and burdened with large rucksacks, the van-guard of an army of long-distance pilgrims engaged on a mission. This was due to Tom Stephenson who included Malham in his itinerary of the Pennine Way which had been officially opened at a mass meeting of ramblers on Malham Moor in 1965. As Malham's economy has profited by a growing invasion of sightseers, its appeal to the quiet traveller has declined inversely. Winter week-days, not summer weekends, are the best time to appreciate Malham.

Malham is not more attractive than a dozen other Dales villages that have retained a quiet and undisturbed privacy. Malham excels because it has within easy reach the most spectacular natural landmark in the north of England: the stupendous limestone cliff of Malham Cove, a compulsive magnet that draws all active visitors to the village. And all around are emerald hills jewelled by crowns and necklaces of virgin white, lovely waterfalls and mischievous streams that play hide and seek: these are the delights that make Malham so special.

Monk Bridge, Malham

THE PIKEDAW CALAMINE CAVERNS

Malham's present industries are tourism and agriculture, mainly sheep farming, but a hundred years ago there was mining for zinc and lead ores on Pikedaw Hill, at an elevation of 1600 feet, north-west of the village; the mine is long abandoned and now is of interest only to the archaeologist, the caver and the curious walker passing nearby.

Two roads head northwards from Malham; the one most in use is that on the west, aiming for Langcliffe in Ribblesdale. It climbs steadily from the village with an oversight of Malham Beck and Malham Cove. When opposite the Cove, a bridleway leaves the road bound for Stockdale and Settle, climbing sharply to pass along the north side of Pikedaw Hill. A more direct but pathless and unauthorised alternative approach may be made from the village, the two routes converging at Nappa Gate beyond Pikedaw Hill.

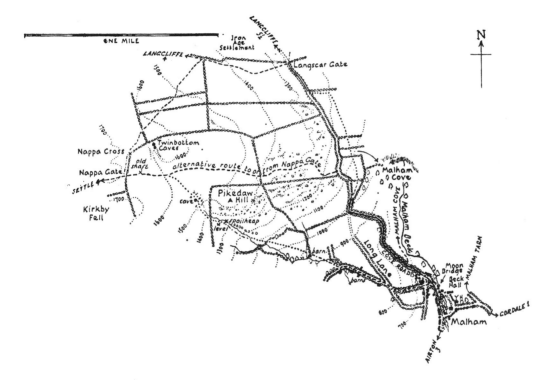

Little of the mine remains to be seen on the surface, the main shaft being sealed with concrete and fitted with an iron trap door but nearby is a mine level with the date 1872 inscribed on the keystone of the arch; a walled cave entrance may also be seen. The wonders of the mine are all underground, half a mile of passages and huge caverns radiating from the bottom of the shaft in all directions.

Another antiquity near Nappa Gate is the ancient Nappa Cross, a wayside relic preserved by incorporation in the wall 200 yards north of the Gate.

OTHER ANTIQUITIES

The road to Langcliffe continues to rise to Langscar Gate where more open ground is reached. Across the moor north-west from this point is the site of a large Iron Age settlement of which only traces remain: a good imagination is needed to visualise the small cultivated fields and hut circles of the primitive occupants thousands of years ago.

On the flat moor north-east of Langscar Gate is the prominent chimney and ruins of a smelt mill where ores of lead and zinc from the small mines on the moor were treated for export to the foundries of industrial Lancashire and Merseyside. An underground flue connected the works and the chimney. Nearby is a stream that disappears into its bed and travels underground for a mile before resurging at the base of Malham Cove.

On the sloping hillside flanking Malham Beck on the east and in view from the Langcliffe road as it leaves the village are the lynchets or cultivation terraces of the early settlers, levelled to ease the growing of crops. The original dividing walls of these allotments can now be barely traced, the pattern having been confused by new walls built two centuries ago. This area of primitive husbandry can be surveyed aerially from the top of the cliffs of Malham Cove.

On the banks of Malham Beck nearer the village was a corn mill long since closed and dismantled. The former industries have gone from Malhamdale. The new one is tourism.

Above *The ruins of the smelt mill*   *Lynchets, Malham Beck*

Above *The approach to Malham Cove*   Overleaf *Malham Cove*

MALHAM COVE

Once seen never forgotten. Even a childhood visit to Malham Cove and never later repeated remains a vivid memory throughout life and is not dimmed by old age. The massive cliffs displayed here, a Colossus of limestone soaring vertically heavenwards out of a green amphitheatre and enclosing it in a gently curving crescent, is an awe-inspiring spectacle, a creation carved by nature on a grand scale. And from an impenetrable cave at its base silently issues the stream last seen on the moor near the smelt mill, its quiet flow contributing to the profound stillness of the scene.

The way to the Cove, trodden by multitudes of sightseers of all ages, leaves the Langcliffe road beyond the last buildings of the village; a path leads down to Malham Beck near the site of the vanished corn mill and follows it upstream in a scattering of trees. The cliff ahead becomes more imposing with every step in an atmosphere of high drama.

When rock-climbing as a sport was in its infancy and a rope was the only aid, limestone cliffs were considered severely out of bounds. The friable nature and smooth texture of the rock, devoid of belays and footholds, added to slipperiness when wet, were considered too dangerous to contemplate ascents. But after the war, as the sport developed and mechanical appliances such as hexes and karabiners and slings became available, making climbing more of a gymnastic exercise, attention turned to the limestone cliffs, and Malham Cove and other cliffs in the area have now a network of routes and a growing clientele.

Above *Limestone pavement above Malham Cove*
Left *The top of the extinct waterfall*

From near the base of the cliff, a path climbs steeply up the west bank of the emerging stream and at the top arrives at a large flat expanse of naked limestone, criss-crossed by a pattern of grikes and cracks, some deep and harbouring ferns and flowers in their sheltered recesses: a botanist's paradise. This natural pavement is easy to negotiate but needs especial care after rain when the surface becomes slippery.

A short traverse along the edge of the cliff, which is not protected by a fence and is dangerous if approached too closely, reveals a steep-sided valley coming down from the north directly to the lowest part of the rim of the cliff, its stream bed well defined but containing no stream. This is Dry Valley, and a simple study of the lie of the land makes it patently obvious that once upon a time it carried a torrent that plunged over the lip of the cliff in a waterfall higher than Niagara. Then gradually over the ages, the soft limestone bed became worn and porous by the friction of water passing over it and the flow diverted to underground channels. It seems reasonable to assume that the stream emerging in Malham Cove is the one that vanished from the valley directly above, but this theory has been disproved by tests of the water. So where does the stream which has vanished from the Dry Valley return to daylight? Read on.

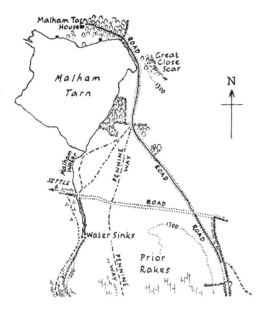

Above *Dry Valley*
Below *Water Sinks*

WATER SINKS

The stream bed in Dry Valley may be followed up on foot, keeping alongside as it trends east and rises to reach open ground. Here is a surprise: the bed, thus far dry, suddenly becomes an active watercourse bringing down a flow from the outlet of Malham Tarn nearby, short-lived because without warning the water disappears from sight amongst a rash of stones. This place is called Water Sinks.

Obviously the stream once flowed overland along Dry Valley and plunged over the precipice in Malham Cove. But, now travelling underground, it has carved a new channel, not yet charted, leading to a daylight resurgence at Aire Head south of Malham village: this is a classic example of the impossibility of conjecturing from the surface the wayward meanderings of subterranean streams.

Malham Tarn from Great Close Scar

MALHAM TARN

Walkers in limestone country soon learn not to expect to find sheets of standing surface water on their wanderings. Even a prolonged downpour of rain is rapidly swallowed by a thirsty bedrock perforated by cracks and fissures worn by the nagging persistence of water. These have become enlarged and extended over the ages into subterranean channels where the rainfall accumulates as rivulets and streams, always seeking faults and weaknesses to progress further.

Some are halted eventually by impervious rock and resurge to daylight, others are condemned to languish forever in underground pools from which there is no escape. The overland streams that find a firm footing between patches of underlying limestone quickly disappear into the nether regions when it recurs. And even limestone that outcrops on the surface becomes waterworn and assumes fanciful shapes ornamented by mosses and lichens and miniature plants. Lovely rock gardens formed by water but holding no water are a constant delight to travellers in limestone areas. The water is below, in grottoes and caverns.

So it is that where the underlying rock is limestone, surface water is absent. There are no tarns or lakes, not even pools and ponds. The Whernside Tarns lie on a bed of rock that, unlike limestone, will not yield. The best and only other example of resistance to water friction is Malham Tarn, an extensive expanse better described as a lake rather than a tarn, with dimensions roughly half a mile square. This sheet of permanent water lies in a shallow basin along a major geological fault on a bed of durable Silurian slate, an oddity in a surround of white limestone scars and outcrops. A happy circumstance of this unexpected transition from a soft substructure to a hard one is that the tarn, sheltered by woodlands, has become a sanctuary for birds and wildfowl which here enjoy a life free from persecution.

Great Close Scar

The direct route for walkers from Malham to the tarn climbs to a pass over a wild moorland on the east side of the Cove and Dry Valley, and crosses the lonely Malham Moor road near the outflow to Water Sinks to continue along the east side of the tarn, passing plantations. Beyond the trees is an unrestricted view of Great Close Scar, directly ahead and high above, its vertical face providing sport for modern rockclimbers.

The private road then turns around the head of the tarn to a fine mansion that seems too grand and out of place in so lonely an environment. This is Malham Tarn House, built in the middle of last century on the site of a former shooting lodge; it has associations with many Victorian literary giants such as Darwin and Ruskin who visited the house as honoured guests. Charles Kingsley wrote his classic *Water Babies* during a stay here. Time brings changes. Now the property is a centre for field studies in the care of the National Trust, and provides tuition and accommodation for parties of students and naturalists, many from overseas.

Malham Tarn House

Past the house a lane leads through a natural woodland, passing the scattered cottages of Water Houses to join a motor road: left for Langcliffe and Malham, right for Arncliffe and Littondale.

Left *Gordale Scar*   Above *Janet's Foss*

GORDALE SCAR

A mile along the road, leaving Malham eastwards, there is a field access on the left leading to a convulsion of nature as awesome as Malham Cove and even more intimidating. This is Gordale Scar where a narrow canyon choked by boulders comes down between towering rock walls hundreds of feet high, sheer and in places overhanging; but, incredibly, they have been 'conquered' by intrepid cragsmen. It is a savage and dramatic scene that would have sent John Ford into a paroxysm of excitement as a location for a Wild West movie. Down the ravine tumbles Gordale Beck in great leaps, the final waterfall plunging over solidified lime deposits, tufa. When, energy spent, the stream flows away sedately, it is augmented by springs along its further course down to the road. Gordale Scar is a petrified monster, gripped in a profound silence that the tinkle of water only serves to emphasise. Other human voices, so often an irritation in quiet places, are here a comfort.

It is possible, but not easy, to climb the block of tufa and scramble, also not easily, amongst the boulders to the top of the ravine where there is evidence of a collapsed cave. This leads to the open moorland above which can be crossed to the Malham Tarn road.

After the harshness of Gordale Scar, a more pleasant diversion is a visit to Janet's Foss. After rejoining the approach road from Malham, a gate on the left admits to a short path into a sylvan setting amongst trees where Gordale Beck, its energy momentarily revived, plunges in a lovely waterfall. This spot was once thought to be a haunt of fairies. A cave on the far bank adds interest to a beautiful picture, better appreciated without the discord of human voices, that refreshes the eyes after their sudden shock at the sight of Gordale Scar.

Aire Head

AIRE HEAD

Malham Beck and Gordale Beck join forces south of the village and are soon augmented by a rising of waters from the depths: the stream that vanished at Water Sinks three miles away here returns to the surface after a long journey in absolute darkness. This place of resurgence is Aire Head and is commonly regarded as the source of the River Aire although Malham Tarn has a better claim to its birthplace. From Aire Head onwards, as though aware of its promotion to the status of river, the young Aire assumes a staid and dignified overland course between wide banks, the antics and excitements of infancy forgotten.

KIRKBY MALHAM

Two miles along the road south of Malham is the ecclesiastical centre of an extensive parish, Kirkby Malham, a small community set in lovely surroundings and disturbed only by the weekend traffic passing through. The venerable old church, dating from the fifteenth century but thought to have been founded a

Kirkby Malham

thousand years ago, stands proudly amongst a scattering of cottages like a hen in the midst of chicks. The interior is interesting, a Norman font bearing testimony to its age, and in the registers is the signature of Oliver Cromwell as witness to a marriage, adding belief to the supposition that the church was used as a garrison for his troops during the Civil War. Another relic of the past is the stocks behind the inn. Roads radiate from the village. The valley road continues downriver to Gargrave, the Settle road leaves here and another crosses the river to Hanlith.

AIRTON

The next village down the dale is Airton, its buildings ranged around a spacious green in the middle of which is a solitary squatter's cottage built long before planning permissions were necessary. Here too, down the road to the river, is a Quakers' burial ground and Meeting House dating from 1700. On the riverside is a large mill, unexpected in surroundings of such pastoral beauty; it is, of course, a forerunner of the many such establishments that flank the Aire as it develops to maturity in the industrial heartland of West Yorkshire. But for a few more miles, the river flows placidly through verdant pastures and lovely woods with the road in close company and pleasant paths and lanes for travellers on foot, all heading for Gargrave.

The approach to Gargrave is heralded by the incessant noise of traffic. The Leeds & Liverpool Canal, here a marina for pleasure craft, is crossed just before the busy A65 highway. The Aire, flowing alongside, bids a sad farewell to pastoral Malhamdale as it follows its destiny reluctantly in the commercial and industrial environment, early exuberance spent.

River Aire at Gargrave

13 OUTLYING AREAS

EAST OF THE THREE PEAKS

Limestone is prevalent but less concentrated in the valleys of Littondale and Wharfedale east of Penyghent where there are caves and potholes galore. My early eager searches for holes in the ground, however, never extended thus far, partly because of the greater distance from home but more especially because on my rarer visits there I found so much else of interest, so much beauty of scenery and so many charming diversions that I was well content merely to wander about and admire the surroundings rather than probe the secret recesses of the limestone escarpments and terraces that grace the flanks of the valleys. In this section of the book, therefore, I will spare readers the details of the underworld of these delectable Yorkshire dales, about which I am not qualified to write, and tell instead about their array of surface delights.

Visitors to the area of the Three Peaks may extend their forays eastwards by any one of four alternative routes.

From Horton in Ribblesdale to Littondale

Travellers on foot (only) may leave Ribblesdale behind by way of Horton Scar Lane, continuing straight ahead on a path when the confining walls end, passing Hull Pot and crossing the open moor beyond before descending to the lonely farmstead of Foxup. Half a mile further on, the hamlet of Halton Gill is reached at the head of Littondale, a pleasant but forlorn oasis that has seen better times when it had a chapel-of-ease, a curate and a larger population. Here the road is joined by another (Route 2 from Stainforth) for the journey down the valley which is a glacial trench watered by the River Skirfare. The next community downriver is Litton, which gives its name to the dale, and two miles further road and river enter Arncliffe, the largest village in Littondale, where Route 3 comes in.

From Stainforth to Littondale

For those in cars, Ribblesdale may be left at Stainforth, a moorland motor road heading north-east from the village and climbing to the depression between Penyghent and Fountains Fell. Here the summit of the pass is crossed by the main Pennine watershed, the domain of the Ribble ending here and all streams beyond being destined for the North Sea. Over the divide, the curious motorist with a large scale Ordnance map will be intrigued by the naming thereon of Giant's Grave and may be impelled to search for this antiquity before continuing his journey to Halton Gill.

From Langcliffe or Malham to Littondale

The crossing from Ribblesdale to Littondale by car may also be made by starting from Langcliffe along the rising road heading to Malham Moor. This initially affords a splendid panorama as it climbs between open verges decorated by outcroppings of limestone, then crosses a depression where Cowside Beck flows placidly unaware of excitement ahead when it plunges over Catrake Force. Then, in wild surroundings, a branch road to Stainforth is passed and a junction reached with the road to Arncliffe in Littondale turning off to the left. This junction may also be reached from Malham by taking the Langcliffe road. A mile along the Arncliffe road at Water Houses, a short detour may be made to Malham Tarn. The road goes on, mile

Above *Darnbrook*

Right *Arncliffe*

after mile and lonelier than ever, to pass the access drive to Tennant Gill where Pennine Way walkers start the long ascent of Fountains Fell. The road then descends sharply into the deep side-valley of Darnbrook Beck, crossing it at the isolated farm of Darnbrook House, and climbing out as steeply for a final high-level sweep across a colourful hillside and a long descent to the relative sophistication of Arncliffe.

Littondale is a pageant of loveliness all along its length and attains near perfection at Arncliffe, its 'capital'. Here the cars of first-time visitors invariably come to a halt alongside the spacious village green, around which are ranged buildings in various styles of rural architecture yet all neatly fitting into a picture of sylvan tranquillity. A short byway leads down to the parish church of St Oswald, an eleventh-century foundation rebuilt and restored. It stands on the banks of the River Skirfare, here crossed by an elegant bridge in a bower of mature trees. It is a beautiful place.

Above *Arncliffe Bridge and church*

Below *Hawkswick*

Visitors interested in relics of the distant past will be rewarded by a walk up the lane alongside the inn at Arncliffe, turning left at the top along the hillside overlooking the village. Here still to be seen are the crumbled walls of an extensive Iron Age settlement, one of many such sites in the district.

Two miles down the dale from Arncliffe is the village of Hawkswick, formerly a possession of Fountains Abbey. Then, with the high confining skylines faltering, Littondale comes to an end as it enters the parent valley of Wharfedale.

Mastiles Lane   Below *Descent into Wharfedale*

Langcliffe or Malham to Wharfedale

The shortest and most direct way from Ribblesdale to Wharfedale is available to pedestrians only although much of the distance can be travelled by car. The road from Langcliffe described in Route 3 can be continued by car beyond the Arncliffe junction and two junctions with motor roads from Malham and the access to Malham Tarn, after which it becomes a bridleway. This is called Mastiles Lane and is joined by another coming up from Malham via Bordley near a fragmented stone circle, and finally, becoming surfaced again, crosses moorland and descends to Threshfield in Wharfedale one mile from Grassington. Unfrequented today, Mastiles Lane was once an active pedestrian and packhorse route, a link between Fountains Abbey and its extensive properties in the Malham area.

WHARFEDALE

Wharfedale forms the eastern boundary of the area described in this book. Of all the Yorkshire valleys, I rate Wharfedale second only to Swaledale, the balance being tipped slightly in favour of the latter because of its quietness and freedom from commercial interests and heavy tourist traffic. But both are beautiful, equally so, and Wharfedale has the greater variety of interests; this is a fact recognised by a weekend flow of visitors from the Yorkshire towns, its easier accessibility adding to its popularity. Wharfedale is better appreciated on weekdays rather than weekends, and best of all appreciated by following the course of the River Wharfe all the way from a prattling babyhood in the rough Pennines to a graceful maturity at Bolton Abbey, a distance measured by a succession of lovely scenes rather than miles. And the transition from wild beginnings to gentle adolescence is most impressive if the tour of the valley is started at Hawes in Wensleydale.

A road leaves the busy street in Hawes heading south and almost at once enters the village of Gayle, not a suburb but an independent settlement since Celtic times and now a centre of Wensleydale cheese-making. The village is picturesque rather than pretty.

Duerley Beck rushes over a rocky bed confined by stout walls between the terraced cottages and below the bridge that carries the road, tumbling in waterfalls in its haste to join the River Ure.

Gayle

The road climbs sharply after leaving Gayle, to the top of a ridge crossed by the grass-grown Roman road from Ingleton to Bainbridge. There follows an even steeper descent into the valley of Langstrothdale, arriving there at a bridge over the youthful Wharfe running in a limestone bed. The road follows alongside and reaches Hubberholme, an oasis of greenery with a church far too large for the sparse population but popular with visitors because of its ancient rood loft, a survival of pre-Reformation times. A pleasant mile onwards, with trees now gracing the scene, is the village of Buckden, its name derived from the deer forest that once existed here; it is reached after crossing a bridge where a tributary comes in from the north-east.

Buckden is not as it was. I remember the village before the war as a place of profound quiet, isolated from the world outside except for a link provided by a daily bus from Kettlewell down the dale, a local service that brought also a few walkers from the towns whose needs were catered for at the Buck Inn. Today, Buckden's emancipation has been completed by a large car park to accommodate a daily influx of visitors who invariably halt here on motoring tours of the Dales; caving enthusiasts come to explore the limestone scars on the hillsides, and on most summer days the inhabitants are outnumbered by strangers who have no roots here but probably wish they had.

Buckden is delightful, the scattered cottages are snugly sheltered between lofty fells and dominated by Buckden Pike in the east. It is a setting of mature native woodlands with a river that here says farewell to the wild surroundings of birth and infancy and sets forth on a long journey down the valley to the industrial heartland of Yorkshire.

Above *Hubberholme Church*
Below *Buckden*

Kettlewell

Two miles down the dale from Buckden the valley road passes between the buildings of Starbotton. This is an old settlement with little scenic distinction to halt through traffic although, like so many rural outposts, it has fallen prey to seekers of weekend and holiday homes.

Two miles further is the large village of Kettlewell, outbid by Grassington as the capital of Upper Wharfedale despite a long history that earned inclusion in the Domesday Survey and close associations subsequently with the monastic foundations in this part of the county. There are shops and hotels and a choice of other accommodation for the many who sojourn here. Other roads coming in make Kettlewell a good centre for motorists, the steep ascent of Park Rash being a prelude to a fine moorland crossing to Middleham and Wensleydale. A secondary road leaves the main road, which here crosses the river, and persists along the east side and makes acquaintance with pleasant villages along the way; and the entrance to Littondale is soon reached along the main road, this side valley having two motor roads over the tops to Ribblesdale. Walkers too have a choice of routes available to them: Great Whernside, overlooking the village, is an obvious target for the more active, and pleasant riverside rambles await the less energetic. In rain, the roomy interior of Dow Cave at Park Rash provides shelter and interest for caving beginners at the cost of wet feet.

170   Kettlewell is a compulsive stop for travellers along Wharfedale.

The main road, now on the west side of the river, is soon joined by the road emerging from Littondale, and in a further half-mile there appears on the right across a rising field a feature that cannot be passed unnoticed and from which it is difficult to avert the eyes. This is Kilnsey Crag, a massive buttress of limestone soaring vertically above the field alongside the road; the crux is a tremendous overhang jutting 15 feet from the vertical and forming a roof over space. Long considered impossible to climb, a first ascent was made in 1956 and a number of routes have been added over the years including the sensational overhang where, with the help of mechanical appliances, supermen have made inch by inch progress, like flies on a ceiling, to arrive triumphant at the top.

Above *Kilnsey Crag*
Below *Upper Wharfedale*

At the hamlet of Kilnsey, for many years the venue of an annual agricultural show, a road crosses the river to the village of Conistone and the quiet back road to Grassington, but the main road continues south, rising at one point to give a classic retrospect of the upper valley known as the Queen's View.

Market Square, Grassington

As the journey continues south, an increase in local traffic heralds a more urban environment ahead, and when wayside cottages are succeeded by suburban houses at the village of Threshfield and along the road going east therefrom there is no doubt that a place of some importance lies ahead. This is Grassington, rooted in Celtic history, mentioned in the Domesday Book. It was once a village concerned mainly with lead mining but, since the closure of the industry last century, it has blossomed exceedingly as a tourist centre. Its development as such was greatly assisted by the arrival of a railway. However, that too was a victim of the postwar motor car, and is now defunct. Traces of antiquity remain in the cobbled market square and the quaint corners and alleys but the emancipation of Grassington into a sophisticated community, now better described as a small town, is complete, a variety of shops and business enterprises catering for the valley's needs, and hotels and boarding houses for an increasing influx of visitors. All roads lead eagerly to Grassington, and those that lead away carry people vowing to return.

Grassington has become the undisputed capital of Upper Wharfedale and its rise in status has been achieved without disfigurement by large industrial complexes, business parks and supermarkets, nor has its development caused any damage or defacement to its intimate rural environs which retain a pastoral charm contributed by fragrant meadows and hedgerows, native woodlands and a lovely river now grown to maturity. Here too the confining hills relent to allow a road to creep over to Nidderdale and another to Skipton; a green bridleway crosses Malham Moor to join a road into Ribblesdale, and there is a network of pleasant paths for walkers.

Trollers Gill near Appletreewick, reached by a minor road south of the town, is a limestone gorge well worth visiting.

Grassington has come of age gracefully.

Two roads resume the journey down the valley in the company of the river, that on the west bank passing the village of Linton, once voted the prettiest in the north and displaying a sundial awarded for the honour. Nearby, a sudden turbulence in the river is caused by a limestone fault crossing the bed and here are Linton Falls.

The two roads come together at Burnsall, two miles further, a neat and compact village, well endowed by nature with a lovely riverside setting supplemented by caring residents who take a pride in maintaining their heritage.

They share their good fortune by welcoming visitors, catering for their comfort in hotels and boarding houses, and providing sporting and recreational facilities with the river, here crossed by a graceful bridge of five arches, a focal attraction; boating and fishing are available and there are delightful riverside walks to Bolton Abbey and Grassington. Why go to Spain?

Burnsall

A few more sylvan miles downriver from Burnsall, by road or footpath, brings into view the stately Barden Tower, built in the proportions of a castle and dating from the fifteenth century. It was the residence of Lord Henry Clifford, owner also of Skipton Castle, and was restored in 1657 by a famous descendant, Lady Anne, a generous benefactress who dedicated her life and her fortune to repairing many churches and castles and bridges in the north-west of the country that had suffered medieval decay.

Nearby, spanning the river, is Barden Bridge, a seventeenth-century arch scheduled as an ancient monument, at a meeting of riverside paths.

Extensive natural woodlands border the road south of Barden and a path leads through the trees to a spectacular highlight in the course of the Wharfe; the river, flowing placidly in a wide bed beneath a canopy of foliage, is suddenly confined to a narrow channel by encroaching rocks on both

Above *Barden Tower*
Below *The Strid*

Bolton Abbey

sides and rushes through in a furious rage. This is the Strid, but let nobody less qualified than an Olympic long jump gold medallist attempt to leap across: there have been casualties amongst those who thought they could perform this feat. It is a place of danger in a scene of unsurpassed beauty.

Finally, this tour of Upper Wharfedale ends, as does the tranquillity so far enjoyed, at a large roadside car park and, on most days, an animated throng of visitors. This popular resort, within easy reach of urban Yorkshire, is Bolton Abbey and the spectral ruins of this twelfth-century monastery have a haunting influence upon the scene. The greater attraction for those who come here, however, is the free and open access to a beautiful stretch of the river and the woodland walks alongside: it is a grand venue for picnics, fun and games, and exciting crossings of the stepping stones.

The Abbey, properly a Priory, was occupied by monks until their proud building fell victim to the Dissolution, its dismantled stones being later used in the construction of Bolton Hall nearby. The nave, however, has been preserved and adapted as the parish church.

Sad are the ruins and sad are the thoughts of those who have followed the course of the river from humble beginnings to majestic splendour and must here say farewell to a charming companion as it recedes into the distance as yet unaware that the best is behind and that soon the friendly hills will be replaced by gaunt factories and workshops, the singing of birds by the drone of traffic, youthful sparkle by drab greyness. Life was happier at Buckden.

WEST OF THE THREE PEAKS

Inland from the volcanic rocks and slates of the southern part of the Lake District, across the alluvial plain of Lyth, there occurs a sudden upthrust of limestone rimmed by west-facing white cliffs in two sections; these are known locally as Scout Scar and Cunswick Scar. Behind these escarpments are extensive heights where occasional outcrops and clints indicate the nature of the underlying rock, but the limestone here is clearly of sterner stuff than that found in the area of the Three Peaks. Despite an above-average rainfall there are no caves, no potholes, no ways into the interior of the mass formed by water action. Nor are there any surface streams, rain falling here sinks immediately, leaving the ground dry, and is emitted as springs around the base. I have long nourished a theory that somewhere in the interior of Scout Scar is a master

Scout Scar

cave containing a subterranean lake which rises and falls according to the weather conditions above and releases its water sparingly in minor springs at valley level. I may be quite wrong in supposing this but the possibility remains. Someday, not in my lifetime, an intrepid caver may find a hole in Scout Scar with a tunnel leading into its heart and its secrets will be revealed, but by then I shall be past caring.

Scout Scar has always been a favourite promenade for Kendal folk, its popularity recognised in recent years by a car park: the cliffedge commands a superb view of the Lakeland fells and the Kent Estuary and, in springtime, of the damson blossom around the farms of the Lyth Valley. A round shelter, erected in 1912 as a memorial to King George V, crowns the highest point.

Scout Scar and Cunswick Scar are the forerunners of a belt of limestone that sweeps around the immediate west side of Kendal; here large quarries have produced the building

Hawes Bridge

material for the older parts of the town, giving it a distinction that merited its description as 'the old grey town' in pre-war and pre-concrete days, a distinction sadly sacrificed, together with much of the town's character, to the whims of modern planners. Below one of the quarries, now disused, is the only known cave hereabouts: Helsfell Cave, amongst trees, yielded up the skeleton of a wolf after a forced entry.

This belt of limestone then appears on the surface only intermittently but is next in evidence about two miles south of Kendal near the village of Natland; here it crosses the River Kent at Hawes Bridge and flanks the river in a deep gorge and provides natural pavements along the banks.

The next surface evidence of limestone in quantity occurs on Farleton Knott, a steep hill skirted by the M6 motorway. Its presence is unsuspected, except at a large quarry burrowing into its lower slopes, until the crest is reached when a pleasant display of scars and outcrops adds a noble crown to a hill not otherwise distinguished. The Knott is best climbed by paths on the easier north side, not by an eroded scramble on its west front. The top is a splendid viewpoint for the Lake District and the sea across the Westmorland plain.

Limestone next asserts itself magnificently in the neighbouring Hutton Roof Crags, overlooking the village of that name; long scars and extensive outcroppings add lustre and sparkle to an interesting landscape. Interlaced amongst the rocks are pleasant rambles enhanced by sweeping views over the wide valley of the Lune to the high skyline of the Three Peaks area beyond.

Summit cairn and limestone pavement, Hutton Roof Crag

Perched precariously on the hillside west of the village of Hutton Roof is the biggest of all the detached limestone boulders I have come across in my travels in the area. Standing 15 feet high, this is not a natural outcrop but has fallen from the slopes above and come to rest on embedded rocks that form a plinth. It is protected from weather erosion by its overhangs.

The village of Hutton Roof is well named. It occupies a plateau to which all roads of approach rise sharply. The parish church, sheltered by mature trees, dates from 1881, succeeding earlier churches on the same site, one preserved stone bearing the date 1601. The war memorial in the churchyard is an uncut block of the local limestone.

Hutton Roof Rakes

Limestone is next seen in the bed of the River Lune at Kirkby Lonsdale, a small market town with many interesting medieval features. The parish church is a Saxon foundation and still retains, despite restorations, good examples of Norman architecture. Most of the many visitors to this interesting old town gravitate to its famous Devil's Bridge spanning the river; it once carried the main highway but has been closed to traffic since the construction of a bypass. This graceful structure of three ribbed arches is thought to date from the late fifteenth century, replacing an earlier one attributed to the Devil.

Continuing east from Kirkby Lonsdale there is a fusion of the impervious limestone, unyielding to weather and water, with its carboniferous cousins on the moors beyond Casterton, described in Chapter 3, which easily succumb – and suddenly excitement becomes rampant.

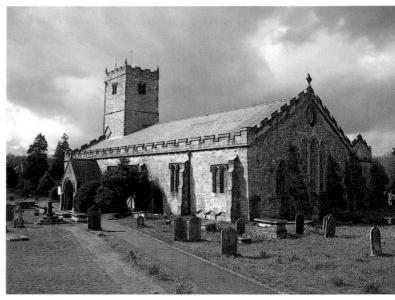

Above *The Parish Church of Kirkby Lonsdale*
Below *Devil's Bridge*

14 THE THREE PEAKS WALK

IT WAS INEVITABLE that someday someone in North Ribblesdale would look around at the three hills that dominate and have their roots in the valley, and suggest that their summits should be linked in a single expedition on foot, a strenuous marathon and a test of endurance and stamina. The idea has been adopted with increasing enthusiasm over the years and the complete circuit has become recognised as a hallmark of ability, those successful being rewarded with an invisible halo.

There are simple rules: the walk must be completed in the course of a day's outing and finish at the starting point, which may be anywhere on the route; the usual preference is Horton in Ribblesdale. I reckon the distance to be 24 miles, although officially it is 20¼, and the total amount of climbing to be around 5000 feet, all of it over rough and undulating terrain. Inevitably, too, some participants have chosen to regard the walk as a race, their concern being to complete the round in record time. This is to be greatly regretted: walking is a pleasure to be enjoyed in comfort. And sadly there are imprints of wheels on paths designed only for boots. In places, to combat severe erosion, protective duckboards cover the crumbling paths. The Three Peaks Walk is a splendid exercise, not an ordeal to be done in a mad rush. For those contemplating the walk, the best advice is to keep going steadily, don't rush, don't give up or you will give up at difficulties throughout life, don't fall by the wayside and, above all, enjoy every mile, especially the last.

Reproduced are the route diagrams I prepared some twenty years ago for my book, *Walks in Limestone Country*: they remain substantially correct subject to a few very minor alterations. References alongside the route refer to the page numbers I have retained from that book.

THE THREE PEAKS WALK

24 miles

The Three Peaks are our old friends, Whernside Ingleborough and Penyghent, which, being flat-topped, are strictly not peaks at all. This collective name for them is too flattering, but there is a fine challenge about it that inspires many walkers to attempt to reach all three summits and make a complete pedestrian circuit in a single one-day expedition. The Three Peaks Walk has become a recognised test of ability and endurance, and in recent years it has attracted increasing attention. Inevitably, and regrettably, it has become the subject of competitive races, both on foot and on wheel, and the breaking of records. With these attempts to accomplish the circuit in double-quick time, stop-watch in hand, we are not concerned here. The intention of this chapter is to detail the walk for the benefit of those whose main object in walking is pleasure and who climb hills for their intrinsic merit, for those who are not too preoccupied with tight timetables to study the landscape as they go along or turn aside to admire a shy saxifrage. Nevertheless, this is an undertaking for strong walkers only; not merely good walkers, but good walkers with staying power. It is a gruelling test of stamina. Many more walkers start the course than finish it. Many fall by the wayside, and some on stony ground.
Happily, it is a walk with few rules. The aim is to link the three summits on foot in a single walk, ending it at the place of starting, which may be any point on the route. Horton in Ribblesdale is most in favour, and the walk is here described as starting from and finishing at Horton Church, in an anti-clockwise direction (as suggested in the leaflet of the Youth Hostels Association, *The Three Peaks Walk*). The detailed maps in this chapter are, however, serviceable whichever starting point is chosen and whichever direction is taken. But there is no set route, each walker being free to plan his own course, in doing which he should respect the laws of trespass and the country code.
Preferably, the walk should be attempted only with foreknowledge of the terrain, acquired on previous outings, and in clear and settled weather. The hours of daylight are too short in winter (never walk on limestone in the dark). 24 miles over rough hills, with nearly 5,000 feet of ascent and, of course, as much descent, is no Sunday School picnic. It is far too arduous a journey for walkers whose performances can only be described as 'fair to middling', but even such tortoises can earn a diluted fame by doing the walk a section at a time over a season, leisurely, and the odds are that they will enjoy the Three Peaks much more than the hares.

THE THREE PEAKS WALK
RECOMMENDED ROUTE

34
(2)

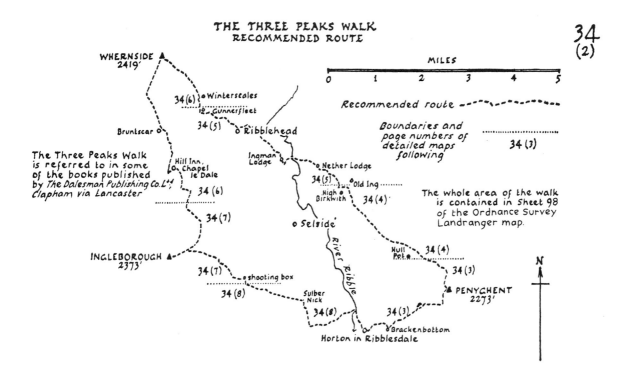

WHERNSIDE
2419'

34(6) o Winterscales

Gunnerfleet

Bruntscar o

34(5)   o Ribblehead

The Three Peaks Walk
is referred to in some
of the books published
by *The Dalesman Publishing Co.Ltd*,
Clapham via Lancaster

Hill Inn,
Chapel
le Dale

34(6)

34(7)

INGLEBOROUGH
2373'

34(7)   o shooting box

34(8)

34(8)   Sulber
Nick

Horton in Ribblesdale

Ingman
Lodge

o Nether Lodge

34(5)   Old Ing

High
Birkwith   34(4)

o Selside

River Ribble

Hull
Pot   34(4)

34(3)

PENYGHENT
2273'

34(3)   o Brackenbottom

MILES

0   1   2   3   4   5

Recommended route ---

Boundaries and
page numbers of
detailed maps
following   34(3)

The whole area of the walk
is contained in Sheet 98
of the Ordnance Survey
Landranger map.

N

34
(3)

The map starting on this page and continuing on the
next following five pages is concerned only with the
Three Peaks Walk. It is given in the form of a continuous
strip, landmarks and features off-route being omitted to
aid clarity, unless they are a help in determining location.
The map gives all the necessary directions regarding gates,
stiles, etc., and should enable the walk to proceed without
hesitation about the correct route and without reference
to other sources of information, but in a few places where
doubts may arise amplifying notes are appended to the map.
The nature of the terrain to be walked is given in side-notes
on each page, with mileages and amounts of climbing.

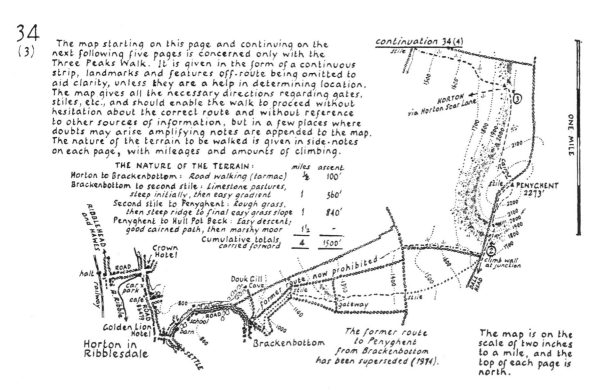

THE NATURE OF THE TERRAIN:

	miles	ascent
Horton to Brackenbottom: *Road walking (tarmac)*	½	100'
Brackenbottom to second stile: *Limestone pastures, steep initially, then easy gradient*	1	560'
Second stile to Penyghent: *Rough grass, then steep ridge to final easy grass slope*	1	840'
Penyghent to Hull Pot Beck: *Easy descent; good cairned path, then marshy moor*	1½	–
Cumulative totals, carried forward	4	1500'

continuation 34(4)

stile

1500
1600

HORTON ←
via Horton Scar Lane

1700
1800
Horton Scar 2000'

2100

3

ONE MILE

stile ▲ PENYGHENT
2273'

2100
2100
2000
1900
1800

RIBBLEHEAD
and HAWES

Crown
Hotel

halt   ROAD

railway

Car
park

café

cafe

Golden Lion
Hotel

Horton in
Ribblesdale

school

barn

SETTLE

800

900

1000

ROAD B6479

Douk Gill
Cave

Former route now prohibited

stile

1100

gateway

1000

1100

1300

DALE HEAD

1400

1500

1600

climb wall
at junction

2

stile

Brackenbottom

The former route
to Penyghent
from Brackenbottom
has been superseded (1974).

The map is on the
scale of two inches
to a mile, and the
top of each page is
north.

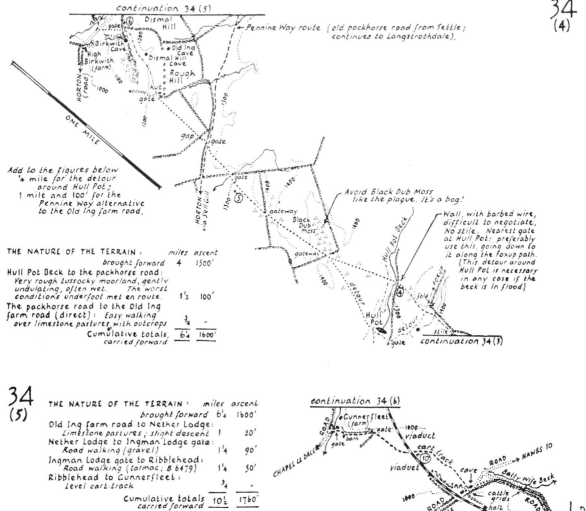

34 (4)

continuation 34 (5)

Pennine Way route (old packhorse road from Settle; continues to Langstrothdale).

Add to the figures below
¼ mile for the detour around Hull Pot;
1 mile and 100' for the Pennine Way alternative to the Old Ing farm road.

Avoid Black Dub Moss like the plague. It's a bog!

Wall, with barbed wire, difficult to negotiate. No stile. Nearest gate at Hull Pot: preferably use this, going down to it along the Foxup path. (This detour around Hull Pot is necessary in any case if the beck is in flood.)

THE NATURE OF THE TERRAIN :	miles	ascent
brought forward	4	1500'
Hull Pot Beck to the packhorse road: Very rough tussocky moorland, gently undulating, often wet. The worst conditions underfoot met en route.	1½	100'
The packhorse road to the Old Ing farm road (direct): Easy walking over limestone pastures with outcrops	¾	–
Cumulative totals, carried forward	6¼	1600'

continuation 34 (3)

34 (5)

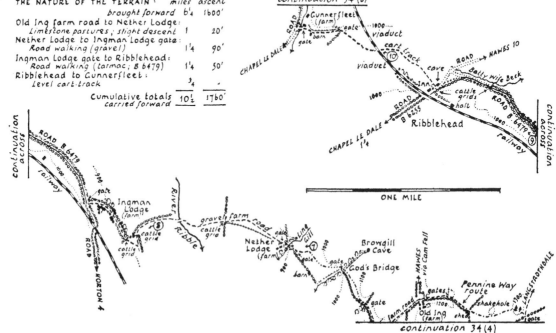

THE NATURE OF THE TERRAIN :	miles	ascent
brought forward	6¼	1600'
Old Ing farm road to Nether Lodge: Limestone pastures; slight descent	1	20'
Nether Lodge to Ingman Lodge gate: Road walking (gravel)	1¼	90'
Ingman Lodge gate to Ribblehead: Road walking (tarmac; B 6479)	1¼	50'
Ribblehead to Gunnersfleet: Level cart-track	¾	–
Cumulative totals, carried forward	10½	1760'

continuation 34 (6)

Ribblehead

ONE MILE

continuation 34 (4)

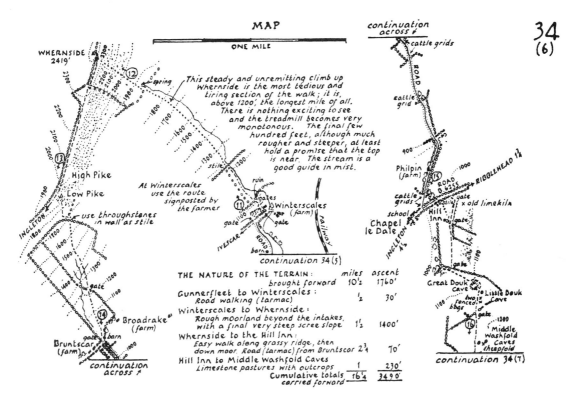

MAP

34 (6)

ONE MILE

continuation across ↑   cattle grids

WHERNSIDE 2419'

⑫   spring

This steady and unremitting climb up Whernside is the most tedious and tiring section of the walk; it is, above 1200', the longest mile of all. There is nothing exciting to see and the treadmill becomes very monotonous. The final few hundred feet, although much rougher and steeper, at least hold a promise that the top is near. The stream is a good guide in mist.

cattle grid

⑬   stile

High Pike

Low Pike

Philpin (farm)   ⑮   RIBBLEHEAD 1¼

At Winterscales use the route signposted by the farmer   ruin   gates   ⑪   Winterscales (farm)   gate

use throughstones in wall as stile   gate   gate   barn

ROAD B 6255   x old limekiln

school   Hill Inn

Chapel le Dale

gate   ⑭   Broadrake (farm)

continuation 34(5)

Great Douk Cave   Little Douk Cave

two fenced bdge   gate

⑯   Middle Washfold Caves

continuation 34(7)

gate   barn

Bruntscar (farm)

continuation across ↑

THE NATURE OF THE TERRAIN:	miles	ascent
brought forward	10½	1760'
Gunnerfleet to Winterscales:		
Road walking (tarmac)	½	30'
Winterscales to Whernside:		
Rough moorland beyond the intakes, with a final very steep scree slope	1½	1400'
Whernside to the Hill Inn:		
Easy walk along grassy ridge, then down moor. Road (tarmac) from Bruntscar 2¾		70'
Hill Inn to Middle Washfold Caves		
Limestone pastures with outcrops	1	230'
Cumulative totals carried forward	16¼	3490'

34 (7)

MAP

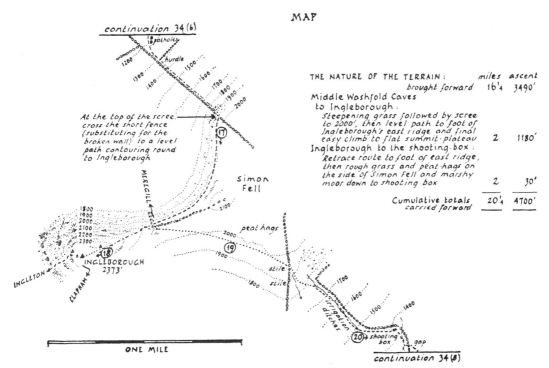

continuation 34(6)   potholes

hurdle

At the top of the scree cross the short fence (substituting for the broken wall) to a level path contouring round to Ingleborough   ⑰

Simon Fell

MERE GILL   peat hags   ⑲

⑱   INGLEBOROUGH 2373'   stile

INGLETON   CLAPHAM   stile

Irrigation ditches

⑳ shooting box   gap

continuation 34(8)

ONE MILE

THE NATURE OF THE TERRAIN:	miles	ascent
brought forward	16¼	3490'
Middle Washfold Caves to Ingleborough:		
Steepening grass followed by scree to 2000', then level path to foot of Ingleborough's east ridge and final easy climb to flat summit-plateau	2	1180'
Ingleborough to the shooting-box:		
Retrace route to foot of east ridge, then rough grass and peat hags on the side of Simon Fell and marshy moor down to shooting-box	2	30'
Cumulative totals carried forward	20¼	4700'

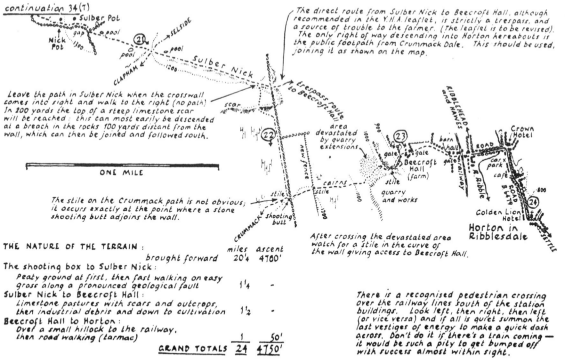

continuation 34(7)

Sulber Pot

gap   pool

Nick   21   SELSIDE
Pot 1500
              pool
       pool   pool   Sulber Nick
            1200
CLAPHAM

The direct route from Sulber Nick to Beecroft Hall, although recommended in the Y.H.A. leaflet, is strictly a trespass, and a source of trouble to the farmer. (The leaflet is to be revised). The only right of way descending into Horton hereabouts is the public footpath from Crummack Dale. This should be used, joining it as shown on the map.

Leave the path in Sulber Nick when the crosswall comes into sight and walk to the right (no path). In 200 yards the top of a steep limestone scar will be reached : this can most easily be descended at a breach in the rocks 100 yards distant from the wall, which can then be joined and followed south.

scar

trespass route to Beecroft Hall

RIBBLEHEAD and HAWES

Crown Hotel

22   area devastated by quarry extensions

new fence   990

1000   23   barn hall   ROAD

gate   gate   gate   railway   car park

Beecroft Hall (farm)   R. Ribble   café

ONE MILE

The stile on the Crummack path is not obvious; it occurs exactly at the point where a stone shooting butt adjoins the wall.

stile

stile   stile   stile

CRUMMACK   shooting butt

1200   1000   quarry and works

Golden Lion Hotel   800   24

Horton in Ribblesdale

After crossing the devastated area watch for a stile in the curve of the wall giving access to Beecroft Hall.

THE NATURE OF THE TERRAIN :	miles	ascent
brought forward	20¼	4700'
The shooting box to Sulber Nick :		
Peaty ground at first, then fast walking on easy grass along a pronounced geological fault	1¼	-
Sulber Nick to Beecroft Hall :		
Limestone pastures with scars and outcrops, then industrial debris and down to cultivation	1½	-
Beecroft Hall to Horton :		
Over a small hillock to the railway, then road walking (tarmac)	1	50'
GRAND TOTALS	24	4750'

There is a recognised pedestrian crossing over the railway lines south of the station buildings. Look left, then right, then left (or vice versa) and if all is quiet summon the last vestiges of energy to make a quick dash across. Don't do it if there's a train coming — it would be such a pity to get bumped off with success almost within sight.

The greatest reward for those who complete the walk within the rules is the inner satisfaction of achievement; but, second to this, tangible evidence of their performance will be provided by the proprietor of the Penyghent Café in Horton in Ribblesdale in the form of a certificate confirming their success.

The Three Peaks certificate

15   THE SETTLE—CARLISLE RAILWAY

THERE CANNOT BE ANY challenge to the claim that the Settle to Carlisle line is the finest example of railway engineering in the country and that it passes through the grandest scenery. The succession of viaducts striding across deep valleys and ravines, the many tunnels burrowing through the wild Pennine hills to maintain negotiable gradients, and the changing panoramic views, make this a spectacular journey. Excitement is increased by the occasional use of steam trains instead of diesel: the Settle to Carlisle line makes grown men little boys again. For many years, the line was under threat of closure, maintenance being costly on a track that for many miles runs at a height of over a thousand feet above sea level. Happily, however, there has recently been a reprieve, a decision that has gladdened the hearts of all railway enthusiasts. The construction of the line in the 1870s took its toll amongst the workers, many of whom, with their wives and children, succumbed to the exposed and wintry conditions to which their shanty huts offered little defence. But they laboured hard and long on a tremendous enterprise that was to prove their memorial. Details of the construction of the line, with plans and illustrations, are well documented in a paperback *How They Built the Settle—Carlisle Railway*, written and published by W.R. Mitchell, 18 Yealand Avenue, Giggleswick.

For readers who do not know the line, the following pages are a photographic portfolio of scenes along the track and from it, in the section between Settle and Kirkby Stephen in the heart of limestone country, a fitting end to a book that has revived many happy memories for me.

The Duchess of Hamilton

Above *Penyghent from Horton in Ribblesdale Halt*
Below *Dentdale from Blea Moor Tunnel*

Dent Station

Above *Rise Hill Tunnel*
Below *Garsdale Station*

Above *Ais Gil Summit*
Below *River Eden and the railway beyond*

Kirby Stephen Station
Opposite *Ribblehead Viaduct*

Beyond Kirkby Stephen the landscapes change, the white flashes of limestone that have characterised the scenery from Settle now giving place to the rich red of sandstone as the railway and the river run side by side along the beautiful Eden Valley to their shared destination, Carlisle.

INDEX